THIS JOURNAL BELONGS TO

A note from the author

If you have been given this journal, or perhaps got it for yourself, you are most likely on a journey to recover from an eating disorder. And if that is the case, I hope this recovery journal guides you through your journey, as well as gives you a space to document your wins and challenges.

You are amazing. The fact you have chosen to give recovery a go and fight your inner demon is something I hope you are proud of. It isn't easy to recover, especially when your eating disorder has been a comfort to you. But acknowledging that it is something you want to get better from is, in itself, an act of bravery.

I hope this journal helps guide you through recovery, and gives you the strength and motivation to challenge yourself beyond what feels comfortable. At times it will feel challenging, and you may want to run back into the arms of your eating disorder. But I have dedicated space to help deter you from running back to old behaviours, and help you form new coping mechanisms that replace the old.

Nobody can recover for you. But it does make it easier to have a place to turn when you are struggling. If you commit to recovery, there is no saying how far you will go and how abundant your life will become.

Em x

Disclaimer and Trigger Warnings

This journal is not a replacement for professional help, and if you find yourself struggling, please seek medical help. This book is based on the experiences of the author, and additional research conducted. This journal represents the opinions of the author and the content within should not be taken as medical advice. The content here is for informational purposes only. While the author makes every effort to ensure that the information she is sharing is accurate, she welcomes any comments, suggestions, or corrections of errors. She encourages readers to do their own research and consult their healthcare provider with any questions or queries.

This journal should not be used in any legal capacity whatsoever, including but not limited to establishing a "standard of care" in a legal sense or as a basis for expert witness testimony. No guarantee is given regarding the accuracy of any statements or opinions made in this journal.

Trigger Warnings: *Eating disorders, weight, BMI, body image, mental illness, mental health, calories*

Contents

Lack of diversity and representation

Therapy only works if you work with it

The glorification of hospitalisation

Are you in control?

You have a life to be well for

Missing your smaller body

Take it one meal at a time

Your questions answered

Identifying the problem

If you have struggled with your relationship with food and your body, weight, shape, and size, then you know just how damaging this can be on your mental health, as well as your life, relationships, your career and education.

Acknowledging you have a problem is the first step in changing it. But for so many of us, denial plays a huge part in our recovery journey. We are flooded with thoughts of I *am not sick enough*, which in itself, is a form of denial. You are denying your current struggles by invalidating them, and telling yourself that your current struggles are only valid if they manifest into something much worse.

Instead of accepting that we have a problem, we tell ourselves that we have to get **worse** before we are allowed to get **better**, and the issues with this are endless.

If you are denying that you are sick enough and deserving of recovery right now, you have probably told yourself that you need to reach a certain goal in order to be sick enough. Maybe you have told yourself that you have to lose x amount of pounds, that you have to be underweight or even develop physical health complications. *I am not sick enough until I reach x kilograms,* or *I am not sick enough until my hair starts falling out.* These goals are incredibly dangerous to both your mental and physical health because you are 1) denying your current struggles 2) postponing your recovery 3) chasing a new level of sickness. But the thing with eating disorders is that they are never satisfied. Your eating disorder may want you to reach a certain weight, but the minute you get to that weight, your eating disorder will tell you that it is simply not enough and you must continue to lose. Every time you reach a 'goal' motivated by the eating disorder, the goalpost moves further away, and you are left feeling just as invalid as you were before you reached the goal.

We are servants to our eating disorders, and we feel as though it is our duty to do whatever the disorder wants us to do. Our rational selves are overpowered by our desire to please the eating disorder. But why?

You are a servant to your ED

Eating disorders control us. We often believe the misconception that *we* are in control when really it is our eating disorder controlling us. If we were truly in control, we would be able to make our own choices about what we ate without guilt or the influence of our eating disorders. If we were in control, recovery would be easy. But we are not in control, and accepting that is a crucial part of your journey to get better.

Recognising when your eating disorder is in control is difficult, but I want you to think about this. Before you had your eating disorder, your choices were controlled by your rational thinking. *I'm on holiday and I want to have ice cream. I'm at the cinema so I want to have popcorn.* These are examples of choices we make when we are not ruled by an eating disorder. If you were to go on holiday and everyone around you was eating ice cream, your eating disorder might tell you not to, or to get the 'safe' option, and would sound something like this. *I am only allowed the lower-calorie ice cream because I will gain weight if I order what I actually want.*

Our eating disorders control us all the time without even realising it. It drowns out what we really want by making us choose what it wants. It is important to **identify** when your eating disorder is controlling you and **accept** that you are not in control.

1. Write down examples of thoughts or choices when your eating disorder made the choice for you. *E.g. When you went out for a meal and didn't order what you wanted.*

The next time you are choosing what or when to eat, or even *if* you should eat, I want you to ask yourself whether that choice is determined by your eating disorder, or by your rational self.

Rational self VS Eating disorder

It can be difficult to know when your eating disorder is in control of your choices. One thing that helps is imaging yourself before you had an eating disorder, and asking yourself what they would have chosen, or how they decided what to choose.

1. Write down a choice your eating disorder has influenced *e.g. what food you ate for dinner, etc*

_____

_____

_____

_____

_____

_____

_____

2. Now write down what you would have chosen as your rational self *e.g. I would have chosen to have pudding*

_____

_____

_____

_____

_____

_____

_____

See a difference? This is how to identify when your eating disorder is influencing your choices. This is key in your recovery journey because you will have to actively go against the choice your eating disorder makes in order to restore rational choice-making and ultimately win over control!

We hear it all the time, *you're not your eating disorder,* but when you are in the depths of one, it feels like you are. Your choices are all governed by it and you feel like it is your purpose to please the eating disorder. We tie ourselves to the disorder and our true selves are lost. We lose interest in things we once loved, we lose our hobbies and passions, and who we truly are is overshadowed by who our eating disorders make us.

One of the incredible benefits of recovery is finding yourself again. A huge part of this journey is rediscovering things you once loved, and finding new things to love. Recovery from an eating disorder is not just about learning how to have a healthy relationship with food, it is so much more.

Who are you without your eating disorder?

Losing your identity to an eating disorder is heartbreaking. Your entire perception of yourself is based on your body, your weight, and how "good" of a servant you are to your eating disorder. One of the reasons so many of us struggle to commit to recovery is how difficult it is to know who we are without an eating disorder, and so imagining a life without it seems impossible.

Having an eating disorder is consuming. All you can think about is food and weight, and specifically, how to lose it. And why is this? In the Minnesota Starvation Experiment (1945) starved a group of men and documented the physical and psychological effects; one of those being food obsession. Our preoccupation with food is a biological response to restriction. When we are restricting and not giving our bodies enough energy, the "hunger" hormone **Ghrelin** is produced more to make us feel hungry, and therefore eat. But that is difficult when you have a restrictive eating disorder. If you are not responding to these hunger signals, your hunger and preoccupation with food will intensify. The more preoccupied with the food you are, the less you are interested in other things that you used to care about and love.

The less you care about things you once loved, the easier it is to focus primarily on your eating disorder. Sometimes it feels like the only thing we have, so trying to recover from it doesn't always sound appealing. This is why it is important to ask yourself who you are without the eating disorder, and who you want to be.

1. What do you wish you did more of?

---

2. What is something you are passionate about?

---

3. If you could do anything in life, what would it be?

---

4. If people were to describe you, what would they say?

---

5. If you were to pick one thing you like about yourself most, what would it be?

You are more than your eating disorder, even when it doesn't feel like it. Recovery involves detaching yourself from the eating disorder identity. At first, this will be difficult and you may feel lost because you won't have your interests and hobbies back, but trust the process. Along the way, you will find out exactly who you are. You won't be the same person you were before your eating disorder, and you won't be the same person before recovery. And while that is difficult at first, it truly is a blessing in disguise. You have the power to become whoever it is that you want to be, and you have the strength and wisdom from all the pain that your eating disorder put you through. Who you become is ultimately up to you, and that is so exciting.

1. Write about the type of person you want to be *e.g. you could write a day in the life of your future self, or just describe that person*

_____

_____

_____

_____

_____

_____

_____

_____

_____

_____

_____

_____

_____

_____

_____

_____

_____

If you are struggling to let go of the eating disorder identity, remind yourself that you are allowed to evolve. You do not have to stay in the same space forever. Your purpose is not to obey your eating disorder, or lose weight. You owe your eating disorder nothing.

The Toxic EX

It helps to think of your eating disorder as a toxic partner. The relationship is unhealthy and you find yourself battling between staying because you love them, and leaving because you deserve better. I think one of the reasons we are scared of recovery is because, whether it's good for us or not, our eating disorder has provided us with some comfort. One of the many reasons we develop eating disorders is because we are using it as a coping mechanism to cope with something in our lives that we find uncomfortable and painful. It helps numb us from feeling what we so badly do not want to feel. And yet, simultaneously, our eating disorders are trying to kill us while destroying our mental and physical health, our lives, relationships, careers, and education in the process. Comfort and pain co-exist in the form of an eating disorder, which is why it is so hard to detach ourselves from it. But imagine recovery like a breakup.

We have to break up with our eating disorders because we know they are not good for us. We know things can't stay the same forever, and yet it is still a painful process. If you have ever been through a breakup, you know just how difficult it can be. You flow through emotions of hate and love and regret. And a lot of the time, you may ask yourself why you ever broke up with them in the first place. This happens at the start of recovery. You are constantly questioning why you did this and if it is worth all the pain and discomfort, but still know it is what you need to do for your health and happiness.

Just like screaming break-up songs at the top of your lungs is helpful, getting mad at the eating disorder is too.

16

1. Write a letter to your eating disorder, or bullet-point, all the ways in which your eating disorder has caused you pain or damaged aspects of your life. GET MAD.

_____

_____

_____

_____

_____

_____

_____

_____

_____

_____

_____

_____

We often tell ourselves that what we are doing to ourselves isn't that bad. But if someone else was in the same position, what would your advice to them be? There is often one rule for others and a different rule for us. *You shouldn't restrict, but I need to.* We believe we deserve less, that we deserve bad things, and that it is okay for us to hurt ourselves and engage in eating disorder behaviours, but it isn't okay for others to do the same.

1. I want you to imagine someone you love being in a toxic relationship. What would you advise them? Would you tell them to stay because they love them, or would you encourage them to leave because they deserve better? Write down what you would tell someone

2. Now write down the same thing to yourself *e.g. I need to recover because I deserve better, and my eating disorder is not good for me.* You don't have to believe it yet, but write it down anyway

_____

_____

_____

_____

_____

_____

_____

_____

_____

_____

_____

_____

_____

_____

_____

_____

_____

_____

_____

_____

_____

_____

The root of the issue

There is one rule for others and a different rule for ourselves. This double standard is highlighting how we do not see ourselves as deserving as other people. Eating disorders are often symptoms of our belief systems e.g. *I am a bad person, I do not deserve good things, I deserve pain.* We can eat all the food in the world but if we do not address **why** we feel the way we do, and what causes us to act on eating disorder behaviours, then it will be hard to overcome it for good. Imagine garden weeds. You can pull at them, but they will always grow back unless you pull up the root of the plant. Recovery works the same way. If you do not find the root of your eating disorder, the root of your self-destructive behaviours, then the issues will forever come back.

There is a way to discover why you act upon behaviours, and all it takes is asking yourself **why.** Everyone's reasons will be different. But more often than not, there is always a deeper reason for the way we behave and think. We have belief systems about ourselves and if you are prone to self-destruction, it is likely your core belief about yourself is negative.

1. Fill this out based on your behaviours and thoughts and see what your core belief is. It is important to discover this so you can work on accepting it, and changing it.

```
behaviour:



```

↓

why?

```



```

↓

why?

```



```

↓

why?

```



```

Core beliefs about ourselves are usually shaped by the way we have been treated, made to feel, or how we have interacted with our environment. Usually, we can identify an experience which formed our belief about ourselves. This might be that you were invalidated as a child, you were emotionally or physically abused or neglected, or you were taught to internalise shame. It may sound far-fetched relating childhood issues or experiences to an eating disorder, but most of the time, eating disorders are not caused by food itself, but by the way we see ourselves. That is why it is important to get to the root of the issue, so we can accept and work towards healing this part of us.

1.   Write about an experience that influenced the way you view yourself

It's not about food

Eating disorders are a form of food-hyperfixation, whether that be restriction, bingeing, etc. But more often than not, eating disorders are not about food itself, but rather the relationship a person has with oneself. What does this mean? Well, our relationship with food and our eating habits are a reflection of our relationship with ourselves. If we are attempting to avoid a painful memory, experience or thought, we use food as a distraction. Whether we are eating too little or bingeing on food, it is often an attempt to numb and punish ourselves.

When we are overwhelmed with difficult things, or feel a loss of control in our lives, we tend to control food to numb our emotions. We believe that if we cannot control something in our lives, whether it be a traumatic experience, death or bereavement, or the overwhelming challenges of daily life, then we can restore a sense of control by engaging in our eating disorders. But as I have previously stated, we are not the ones in control. However, we attempt to restore some control in an area of our lives that we **can** control: our weight, our intake, and our daily movement. To many others, this may look like a superficial issue with food and weight, but it is not. It is easy for people to misunderstand eating disorders if they have not experienced the reality of one themselves. But to the sufferer, it is an internal storm and a battle every single day. The stereotypes and misconceptions people have of eating disorders can leave us feeling misunderstood and invalidated because while we deal with inner conflict, people on the outside can only see a person struggling with food. It can be incredibly frustrating when people tell us to *just eat,* especially because we do. We do eat. And the belief that we do not is damaging and stereotypical. It leaves us feeling invalid and ashamed of what we eat, and can encourage us to eat in private and develop a huge amount of shame about what we eat. This can lead to us being selective with what we eat, as well as how much. It is common for sufferers of restrictive eating disorders to begin to fear food, and attempt to eat foods that they deem 'safe'.

Fear foods and Safe foods

This isn't something that everyone will experience. Not everyone with an eating disorder is the same and will experience the same symptoms and side effects. But one common symptom of an eating disorder is fearing specific foods, and finding other foods 'safe'.

What makes specific foods fearful? The answer to this differs from person to person, but more often than not, the reason why people fear specific food or food groups is entirely irrational. Our favourite foods may become "off limits" and avoided because we often fear eating "too much". If we avoid our favourite foods, we believe we are stopping the opportunity of over-indulging in this food and gaining weight. This isn't always the case, keep in mind that everyone is different. Another reason a food may be feared is because of the belief that specific foods will make us gain weight or fat. One of the many reasons we may believe this is because of diet culture. Diet culture has been around for decades and has had a huge impact on the way we look at food. Diet culture is everywhere and is often unavoidable. The belief that cake is fattening and salads are the superior lunch option is universally shared, and it is especially hard when you struggle with an eating disorder to not let these beliefs affect us. We may adopt diet culture rules and beliefs and label foods as good and bad. This comes into play when we are talking about fear foods. If a food is universally acknowledged as a 'bad' or fattening food, then we might avoid it in an attempt to control our weight.

Similarly, we might have safe foods. This includes foods that we deem safe to eat because of different reasons. Maybe they are low in calories or fat content, or maybe they promote weight loss as diet culture and our eating disorders would have us believe.

It is important in recovery to not only challenge your fear foods but to challenge the logic behind the fear. Instead of just eating cake, ask yourself why you find cake scary, then challenge the logic. A specific food won't change the way you look, and avoiding that food is far more unhealthy and harmful than eating it.

Reframing the way we look at food is so important in recovery. No food is inherently good or bad for us unless we have an allergy to it, it is mouldy or poisonous.

1. Write down a food you are scared of eating

—————————————————————————————————————

2. Write down why you are scared of eating this food

—————————————————————————————————————

3. Write down a rational response and challenge the fear

—————————————————————————————————————

Whenever you find yourself avoiding a specific food, try and rationalise it and see it as neutral. This food is neither good nor bad and has no power over you.

It is **normal** and expected in recovery for you to crave all the foods you avoided. When you have restricted, it is especially common for you to crave carbohydrate-rich foods because the neurotransmitter Neuropeptide Y (NPY) is elevated. I know for a lot of people who struggle with an eating disorder, eating 'bad' foods or foods diet culture deems unhealthy can often be uncomfortable mentally, and it might bring about shame and guilt. It is important to remember that you are not weak for eating what you crave. In fact, you are strong.

What is healthy? Well, diet culture makes us believe that health involves lots of green vegetables and fruits, organic whole foods, and limiting foods that are 'bad' for us. That is not what health is. Health when it comes to diet is all about balance. The phrase 'eat in moderation' is restrictive and shouldn't be encouraged in recovery from a restrictive eating disorder. This is because, in recovery, there will be times when you will experience strong cravings for certain foods, especially the foods you restricted. To eat these foods in moderation would imply that you have to stop when it becomes 'excessive', which is ultimately restricting if your hunger is not satisfied. The phrase 'eat in balance' encourages all food groups, and all types of foods, and allows for fluctuations in cravings without limiting you to how much is allowed.

One thing that you must know is the importance of accepting your cravings, and honouring them. Accepting that you are craving specific foods can be difficult, especially if these foods are not safe for you, or deemed unhealthy or bad. But accepting that this is your biological and psychological response to restriction is key. There is nothing wrong with your cravings or your hunger. In fact, it is completely understandable why you are experiencing them. Try not to tie emotions to these cravings or foods. All foods are neutral.

Challenging your fear foods

When facing a fear food, it is important to know that the anticipation is the hardest part, and you will eventually feel relief from the fear. You may have thoughts discouraging you from trying the food, but I want you to know that nothing bad is going to happen when you eat this food. This food has been created to aid your life and your body, not punish you or change the way you look.

Write down a fear food of yours. Write down how it made you feel, and rate the fear on a scale of 1-10 before you try the food, and after. Hopefully, you will see the score go down after you have eaten the food. You have two templates to use, but if you find this helpful, I recommend creating your own template on a piece of paper to help you every time you challenge yourself.

Today I am challenging _____ ♡

What scares you about this food?

FEAR BEFORE __/10

_____
_____
_____
_____
_____
_____
_____
_____
_____
_____
_____

How do you feel after eating this food

FEAR AFTER __/10

_____
_____
_____
_____
_____
_____
_____
_____
_____
_____
_____

Today I am challenging _____ ♡

What scares you about this food?

FEAR BEFORE __/10

_____

_____

_____

_____

_____

_____

_____

_____

_____

_____

How do you feel after eating this food

FEAR AFTER __/10

_____

_____

_____

_____

_____

_____

_____

_____

_____

_____

Today I am challenging _____ ♡

What scares you about this food?

FEAR BEFORE __/10

_____
_____
_____
_____
_____
_____
_____
_____
_____
_____

How do you feel after eating this food

FEAR AFTER __/10

_____
_____
_____
_____
_____
_____
_____
_____
_____
_____

Today I am challenging _____ ♡

What scares you about this food?

FEAR BEFORE __/10

_____

_____

_____

_____

_____

_____

_____

_____

_____

_____

How do you feel after eating this food

FEAR AFTER __/10

_____

_____

_____

_____

_____

_____

_____

_____

_____

Today I am challenging _____ ♡

What scares you about this food?

FEAR BEFORE __/10

_____
_____
_____
_____
_____
_____
_____
_____
_____
_____

How do you feel after eating this food

FEAR AFTER __/10

_____
_____
_____
_____
_____
_____
_____
_____
_____
_____

Today I am challenging _____ ♡

What scares you about this food?

FEAR BEFORE __/10

_____

_____

_____

_____

_____

_____

_____

_____

_____

_____

How do you feel after eating this food

FEAR AFTER __/10

_____

_____

_____

_____

_____

_____

_____

_____

_____

_____

Am I sick enough?

As I mentioned before, one of the greatest obstacles in recovery is not feeling sick enough. We let this be a hindrance to our recovery by telling ourselves that only when we are sick enough, we deserve to recover. The idea that we have to be at our worst before we can get better is the very reason so many of us struggle for years of our lives, postponing recovery because we never reach a point where we think *this is enough, i am sick enough.* We tell ourselves once we reach a goal, we will feel sick enough. But when you do reach that goal, it only leaves you feeling just as invalid as before.

There is no sick enough. If there was, you would have recovered a long time ago. If sick enough existed, there wouldn't be people losing their lives to this illness, or spending their entire lives battling it. There will never be a weight that gives you the feeling you are searching for, and yet you still find yourself chasing it. What if I told you that you are chasing your shadow?

There is a huge difference between **being** sick enough, and **feeling** sick enough. Being sick enough started the second you started to struggle with your relationship with food. You were sick enough before you lost a pound. The thoughts you were experiencing were symptoms of an eating disorder, and yet here you are still trying to prove that you are sick enough through your physical actions. Your actions do not determine the severity of a mental illness, and never will. You are chasing a feeling that won't come by changing your body, shape, weight or size. That feeling you are searching for, the feeling of *sick enough*, is only attainable from within. You can lose no weight

37

at all, or you can lose lots of weight, and still, that would not change the fact that YOU ARE SICK ENOUGH JUST AS YOU WERE, AND JUST AS YOU ARE.

Our definition of sick enough is constantly being adjusted to be something we have not yet attained. It isn't something tangible, something you can physically "achieve", it is an inner state. And as hard as it is to accept, you won't **feel** sick enough. You **are** sick enough, but you won't **feel** sick enough.

Stop waiting for the day you feel sick enough to recover. That day will never come for as long as you are engaging in your eating disorder. In fact, you will only see how truly sick you are when you recover. Your mind is plagued by an illness, and so only when you begin to heal and recover will you be able to see yourself and your illness for what it was, and what it is.

Your future is your choice

You can't outgrow an eating disorder with age. It requires a period of recovery to get better, and that is unavoidable. The consequences of not recovering are terrifying, and yet we are more terrified of recovery than we are of what our lives will be like if we never recover.

We are often focused on one day at a time. What we eat today, how much we move today, our weight today, etc. We often forget to zoom out and take a look at the bigger picture. Say you are going to live until you are 90, what will the rest of your life look like?

There are two outcomes: you recover or you don't. It is important to imagine what our futures will look like if we choose to recover, and if we choose not to recover. If you recover, it is hard to pinpoint exactly what your future will look like, because the options are endless. But imagining your future when you do not recover is actually very scary. You know what day-to-day life is like consumed with an eating disorder. There is very little else you do besides think about food. Your days all blend into one, fatigued and unable to do anything fulfilling. You can't join in on the fun, you dread going out because of eating out, and every hour feels like ten because you are just waiting for time to pass between meals. Whatever the reality of your eating disorder is, that is what I want you to imagine when you think of your future. This is, of course, if you do not recover.

1. Write down a summary of your future if you do recover

2. Write down a summary of your future if you do not recover

Which version sounds better? I know it is daunting to think about the future when you are struggling, but it is important that you realise what not recovering looks like. Your dream future is waiting for you, it just requires your commitment to recovery.

Commitment is your best friend

From time to time, you will get bouts of motivation to recover, to eat whatever you want, and feel strong for doing so. But motivation runs out. Recovery is something you have to choose every single day over and over again, and you cannot rely on motivation to get you through.

Commitment to recovery is the most promising way to get through it. But what is the difference between commitment and motivation? Motivation sounds like *screw the eating disorder, I am going to eat whatever I want and get my life back,* but it is only fleeting. Commitment sounds like *even though the eating disorder thoughts are strong today, I am still going against them because I know I need to, even if I don't want to.* This is much more reliable.

Committing to recovery is important. It means that no matter how strong the thoughts are, you act upon recovery behaviours because you know that you need to.

But there is no point in committing to recovery if you find yourself not wanting to recover.

You have to want recovery

This sounds quite daunting when you are struggling, afraid of recovery and comfortable with engaging with your eating disorder. But like anything in life, you have to want it more than you fear it. Of course, both fear and desire can co-exist and **will** for the beginning part of your recovery, but the **want** has to be there too.

1. Write down why you want to recover

_____

_____

_____

_____

_____

_____

_____

_____

_____

_____

_____

_____

_____

_____

_____

_____

_____

2. Write down all the things you want to do that recovery will bring you

_____

_____

_____

_____

_____

_____

_____

_____

_____

_____

3. Write down some goals that have nothing to do with your eating
    disorder

_____

_____

_____

_____

_____

_____

_____

_____

_____

_____

Having goals that aren't related to your eating disorder will be very helpful in your recovery journey. You cannot achieve what you want in this life if you are being controlled by an eating disorder. You won't have the energy, the motivation, the concentration abilities or the desire to achieve. Creating goals will help keep you going through this journey. It is important to imagine your future in recovery and when you are recovered, so always keep an eye on the bigger picture. The choices are endless.

Taking the first step towards recovery

There is never a wrong time to recover. We might tell ourselves that *we have to get worse before we can recover*, but if you were to get worse, that will only make recovery much more difficult. You are deserving of getting better and healing no matter what.

Maybe you want to recover, but don't know how. It can be very intimidating and confusing knowing what to do to initiate recovery, so have a go at these activities!

1. Write down a list of your eating disorder behaviours *e.g. calorie counting, etc*

_____

_____

_____

_____

_____

_____

_____

_____

_____

_____

_____

_____

_____

You have to overcome the behaviours you have listed. Whatever it is that you have listed is keeping you trapped in your eating disorder, so has to go.

How to stop disordered habits

Calorie counting:

Calorie counting is extremely common, and extremely detrimental to your mental and physical health. Your body knows how much it needs better than your eating disorder does and better than diet culture does. We live in a society where calorie counting is encouraged, with calories listed on menus in restaurants. It makes it incredibly difficult to stop this disordered behaviour when we live in a society that encourages it. But it is crucial that you stop counting calories in order for you to learn what your actual bodily needs are, as well as neutralise your relationship with food. Telling yourself that you are only allowed a maximum amount of calories is denying your hunger cues and your bodily needs, and will ultimately lead to energy depletion and an inability to respond to hunger cues.

Whether you're counting calories using a tracking app or mentally calculating them, there is a way to stop. We think that if we stop counting our calories, we will lose control. But remember, we are not in control to begin with, our eating disorders are.

1. Write down how calorie counting has impacted your life

_____

_____

_____

_____

_____

_____

_____

_____

_____

_____

_____

_____

_____

2. Write down what your fears are about not calorie counting

_____

_____

_____

_____

_____

_____

_____

_____

_____

_____

_____

_____

Counteract your irrational fear with a rational response.

If I stop calorie counting, I will...

_____

_____

_____

_____

_____

This is your eating disorder talking and controlling you. But within you, you also have a rational voice that knows better. I want you to channel your rational voice and counteract the fear. *e.g. I won't lose control if I stop calorie counting because I was never in control to begin with. By not calorie counting, I am taking back control from my eating disorder and allowing myself to neutralise my relationship with food, and stop myself from seeing food as a number.*

If I stop calorie counting, I will...

_____

_____

_____

_____

_____

So, how do you stop calorie counting?

Now that you have an answer as to how calorie counting has affected your life, you should be able to see how this behaviour is unhealthy and damaging to you. Acceptance is key in overcoming anything.

49

Tip #1 : Go cold turkey

This is scary, but I want you to tell yourself that from now on, no matter what time of the day it is, you will not purposefully count your calories. This means tracking them and reducing the mental maths. Going cold turkey means immediately stopping the physical act of the behaviour. Instead of drawing out the process, it allows you to immediately stop it to break the cycle. While there may be some mental maths going on, that will go away with time.

Tip #2 : Delete your tracking apps

If you have a calorie tracking app, you should delete it as soon as possible. It can be habitual to log your calories on an app, so deleting it stops the cycle you have been stuck in for far too long. That app has no purpose for you and you are not *out of control* for deleting it. In fact, you are more in control if you delete it. Why do you have to see how many calories you are eating? Seriously, ask yourself how this is impacting your life. Is it stopping you from honouring your hunger, joining in on meals that you have not tracked, or going out and enjoying food spontaneously? Yes.

Your body will require a LOT of energy in recovery. I will talk about this a bit more later.

Tip #3 : Sabotage the maths

If you are counting calories in your head as you go along the day, one thing that is very helpful is sabotaging the maths. What this involves is eating foods throughout the day that you do not know the calories of. This could look like eating an unmeasured spoonful of peanut butter, or drinking juice without measuring it out. It may look like having a few pieces of chocolate. By not knowing the exact calories in these specific foods/drinks, you won't be able to accurately calculate your calories consumed and so the act of counting your calories will become less appealing to you given that the number won't be accurate.

Tip #4 : Try new foods and drinks

In recovery, it is necessary that you try new foods and drinks in order to help you overcome the fear of the unknown (unknown calories, unknown macros, unknown ingredients). I challenge you to order a takeaway or go to a restaurant and order something you haven't gotten before. If the calories are on the menu, ask someone you are with to read the menu out to you or ask the restaurant for a calorie-free menu. This allows you to choose something you do not know the calories of.

Exposure is key. When we fear something, the most effective method to overcome that fear is to expose ourselves to it. If you fear eating something that you do not know the calories of, then this exercise will be very helpful to you.

Why should we stop calorie counting?

Calorie counting underestimates our actual energy needs. Your body works tirelessly to function every single day, and even when you are resting, sleeping, and not doing anything, your body is using lots of energy. Now, if you have restricted your calories or only allow yourself a maximum amount of calories, this is not giving your body the energy it actually requires. The only way to know how much energy your body requires is by listening to your hunger cues, cravings, your energy levels, and appetite. But if you have an eating disorder, your understanding of these factors will be wrong. If you have been ignoring your hunger cues, not honouring your cravings and are in a calorie deficit, you won't be able to tell what your body actually needs. We believe that we only need the bare minimum of calories to function, but that couldn't be more untrue. If you have struggled with a restrictive eating disorder, the amount of energy you need will be much greater than the energy required by a person who has not experienced an eating disorder. You have to remember that your body has most likely been in an energy deficit for a long period of time, and so it will require a lot of energy to repair any internal damage caused by malnourishment and/or energy deficits.

The oxygen analogy

Imagine you are in a running race. You are sprinting towards the finish line. When you cross the line, you are able to stop running and all of a sudden you are struggling to catch your breath. You have to breathe deep inhales at a much faster rate to catch your breath back. That is because sprinting creates an oxygen debt, and when you stop running. your body is attempting to repay this oxygen debt by trying to inhale as much oxygen as possible before your breath returns to normal. This is the same with restriction. When you are restricting for a period of time, you are creating an energy debt. When you stop restricting, you will require a lot of energy to repay this energy debt. This means you have to be eating a lot of food to pay off the energy debt. Only when you have paid off the energy debt will your calorie needs return to "normal". This may take months or years to do but is completely normal and necessary.

By counting calories in and out of recovery, you are disregarding your body's need for lots of energy in order for it to repair what restriction has damaged.

But what is damaged as a result of restriction? Your muscle mass and organ size decrease by up to 20%, resulting in a loss of bone density leaving you more prone to injuries and osteoporosis. As your basal metabolic rate (BMR) is dependent upon your muscle and bone mass, the loss of muscle mass will ultimately lower your BMR, "slowing down" your metabolism. Additionally, starvation can cause the death of cells due to a lack of glucose stores, so your immunity is weakened. Your body struggles to regulate temperature, your kidney function impairs and your body salts, vitamins and minerals are unbalanced. There is a low production of reproductive hormones, your period may stop or become irregular, and there is an increased chance of infertility. You may find that your resting heart rate decreases, but experience postural tachycardia which causes you to feel light-headed or even faint when you stand up. Restriction can lead to cardiac arrest, and worse, death.

So it is vital that you do not underestimate the effect of restriction on your body. You are not an exception to the devastating effects, and the faster you begin recovering, the lower your chance of developing life-long complications.

1. Write down why calories are important to you and why eating enough is necessary

_____

_____

_____

_____

_____

_____

_____

_____

_____

_____

Weighing yourself:

If you struggle with weighing yourself, you are not alone. If you struggle with this behaviour, you know all too well just how addictive it can be, and how detrimental it can be. Weighing yourself allows you to see how the foods you have eaten in the space of 24 hours, and the movement you have done, has impacted your weight. But the truth is, food and movement are only two of many factors that determine your weight. Daily fluctuations are very common and you will never be able to control your weight directly because many of the factors affecting your weight are internal, with your hormones being the most significant.

It is important to understand that you are not in control of your weight to help relieve the anxiety that encourages us to weigh ourselves every day. For sufferers, weighing ourselves daily gives us an idea of how much we are *allowed* to eat on a given day, or how much movement we *should* do. But this behaviour is incredibly unhealthy and only reinforces the idea that your weight controls you.

1. Write down why you weigh yourself (if this applies to you)

Weight is the force of gravity exerted on an object. It is as simple and insignificant as that. And yet, we let it dictate our worth. It is difficult to overcome a fixation on your weight when we live in a society driven by weight loss. But when you break it down, weight is a case of physics. If you are weighing yourself, you are making it difficult to detach your worth from your weight, which is something you will have to do along your recovery journey. Knowing your weight gives it power over you, so I have some tips to help you stop weighing yourself.

Tip #1: cold turkey

Just like calorie counting, you have to go cold turkey on weighing yourself. At first, it will be uncomfortable and you may feel compelled to step on the scale, but don't. You are taking back control. You can do it, even when you don't feel like you can. Yes, the eating disorder may give you a hard time, but it will because it doesn't want what is best for you.

Tip #2: bin the scales

If you can, get rid of them. Not having them in your home makes it easier for you to overcome this destructive habit because even if you wanted to weigh yourself, you can't.

Tip #3: Hide the scales

If you can't bin the scales due to other people in the house needing them, hide them. Ask someone in your home to hide them or put them in a place where you won't be able to easily access them. When weighing yourself becomes a habit, it is easy to go along with the steps in your routine, including weighing yourself in the same position every day. So, move the scales, bin them, and get someone to hide them, they serve you no purpose!

You are more than your weight. Your eating disorder is valid no matter what you weigh. I know it can be hard to gain weight, but I want you to know that your eating disorder does not become less important the more weight you gain. In fact, a sufferer can struggle just as badly at a bigger weight than they did at a smaller weight. You are valid no matter what your weight is.

1. Try a day without acting upon eating disorder behaviours, and use this space to journal how it made you feel.

Let's talk about weight gain

If you have suffered from an eating disorder that has caused you to lose weight, you will have to gain weight in recovery. You are not an exception, and you can't continue telling yourself that you can make a full recovery without gaining weight. We often tell ourselves lies. *I can maintain this weight and recover.* It is a form of denial and it is denying your body and mind true healing. When you have a fear of something, exposure to that fear is the most effective method of overcoming it. If you have a fear of weight gain, you will have to expose yourself to that.

We've talked about belief systems and how they are embedded in our minds. But how do they relate to our fear of weight gain? I want you to ask yourself why gaining weight is scary for you. Dig really deep, and don't dabble on the surface level. It isn't about wanting to look thin, it goes much deeper than that. Maybe you are scared to gain weight because you lack confidence about who you are in your most natural form. Maybe you are scared to gain weight because someone has made a comment about your natural body that insinuated your weight made you less than others. Maybe you are scared to gain weight because you don't feel beautiful. And why is this? Whatever your reason for being afraid to gain weight, I want you to go deeper than you ever have before.

1. Write down why you are afraid to gain weight. Get deep.

We live in a society where fat is frowned upon, and thin is glorified. But the reality is, it doesn't matter what your weight is, your body can still do the exact same thing. You have to work towards body neutrality. This means that you do not love or hate your body, but appreciate your body for what it does. Eating disorders encourage us to harm our bodies in many dangerous ways, and often we don't realise the impact our actions have on our bodies. Let's take a moment to apologise to our bodies, and practise seeing them as our homes. Your body is your home, it has kept you alive for all these years and it's only care is you. It needs nurturing like a plant.

1. Write an apology letter to your body

There will come a time in your recovery where you appreciate the weight you have gained. You will realise how the weight you have gained has allowed you to do so much with your life, and has allowed you to feel energised and genuine happiness. Weight gain is a beautiful thing that allows us to live more comfortably, safer, and happier. It takes some time to get to this point of realisation, but keep going, because I promise there will come a day in your recovery where you are more appreciative of weight gain than you fear it.

1. Write a list of ways your body helps you

How to make weight gain more comfortable

Gaining weight is inevitable. You cannot expect your body to stay the same forever, especially when it has been forced smaller due to restriction and other destructive behaviours. So how can we make weight gain easier and more comfortable for ourselves?

Tip #1 : Wear comfortable clothes

Donate any clothes that no longer fit you to a charity. It can be incredibly triggering to try on clothes that used to fit you, to find that they no longer do. Sizing up in clothes (multiple times) is a part of the recovery journey, and when that day comes, you have to make it as easy as possible for yourself. Try to avoid connecting emotions to it. Instead of thinking *I am so sad I have gained weight*, try to think *these clothes no longer serve me*. Our language is incredibly important during recovery. You have to try and refrain from making judgmental comments about your food, weight, or size, and use more neutral language that detaches emotion from these things.

Tip #2 : wear oversized clothes

If you struggle with feeling comfortable in fitted clothes, don't force yourself to wear them. People find it easier to wear oversized clothes because it allows you to go through the day without being hyper-focused on your body. This is a short-term solution because there will come a day when you will have to accept the body you have grown into.

Tip #3 : Remind yourself why this is a good thing

Weight restoration is necessary. It cannot be avoided in recovery, so try to make it as easy as possible for yourself by reinforcing the positives about it.

1. Write down why it is okay for you to gain weight

_____

_____

_____

_____

_____

_____

_____

_____

_____

_____

_____

Tip #4 : Stop body-checking

Body-checking is a very common behaviour in eating disorders. It allows you to stay hyper-focused on your body and makes it harder to accept change. To make weight gain more comfortable, avoid looking in mirrors if you feel it will trigger you. Cover your mirrors, or try your best to walk past any without spending a few seconds staring at your body in them. Body-checking may leave you feeling disappointed and upset that you have gained weight, so it is best to avoid doing so. Remember weight gain is a great thing, and it is the best choice.

Tip #5 Affirmations

When your brain is programmed in a specific way, your first thoughts when reacting to weight gain may be negative. But the good news is, we can programme our brains to respond in a different way. It just takes correcting any negative reaction and counteracting it with a positive reaction. Your initial thought may be *I have gained weight, I look awful.* But you can counteract that thought with a more positive and healthy one. *I have gained weight, my body is healing.* Language is key, so speak words of kindness and positivity to yourself, and soon, you won't automatically form negatives about yourself.

Body Image

We all struggle with our body image, but when you have an eating disorder, body image issues are usually exacerbated. You might look in the mirror and see something that doesn't actually resemble what you look like. Your view of yourself is distorted which often makes the eating disorder thoughts worse. The way you think you look may even change several times a day, and that can affect your mood and how much you eat.

1. Write down your perception of the way you look

_____

_____

_____

_____

_____

_____

_____

_____

_____

_____

_____

If people have complimented your body, or commented on the way you look in any shape or form, it probably challenges your own view of yourself. How many times have you had someone comment on your appearance and you disagree with them? When our self-perception is plagued, it makes it incredibly hard to accurately know what we look like, and yet we are so fast to reject any compliment. We think we know what we look like better than anyone else, and yet, how is that when we cannot actually see ourselves?

1. Write down compliments people have made about your appearance

_____

_____

_____

_____

_____

_____

_____

_____

_____

_____

See how your own perception of the way you look differs from those around you?

It is so easy to comment on the things we don't like about ourselves and the things we want to change about our appearance, but how often do we take a moment to appreciate the parts we like about ourselves?

1. Take a moment to talk about parts of your appearance that you like

_____

_____

_____

_____

_____

_____

_____

_____

_____

_____

_____

We live in a society where certain body shapes are put on a pedestal. The desired body shape is constantly changing and it has become a trend to look a certain way. From skinny to curvy, the body ideal changes with the seasons. It is incredibly difficult for everyone because we are all burdened with the pressure of looking a certain way, and yet it is merely impossible to be everything society wants us to be. If we are skinny, we still have to have curves, and if we are curvy, we still have to have a flat stomach. These body ideals are completely unrealistic and harmful to everyone, but especially to people who struggle with eating disorders.

Have you ever felt unaccepted by society for the way your body looks? Have you ever been told that your body shape is odd, or had someone tell you that you should probably lose or gain weight? When you are struggling with an eating disorder, these comments can be very triggering and can easily send someone in a spiral.

So how do you stop letting this affect you? How do we learn to accept our natural body? It is a challenge, and yet it is possible. Self-love seems so out of reach for the majority, because to love ourselves is to go against everything society tells us not to do.

But we are changing the narrative, and it starts with the simple act of acceptance.

When I talk about our natural bodies, I refer to the way our bodies looked before we restricted or started any behaviours that attempted to modify and manipulate our bodies. We have to learn how to accept our natural bodies because they are *us* in their most authentic form. There is nothing wrong with how your body looks, and yet we have been made to feel that our bodies are flawed.

Let's understand why we are constantly being fed the idea that our bodies are flawed. We live in a patriarchal society where women have been viewed as objects for as long as time. Our perception of what is considered beautiful is influenced by eurocentric standards of beauty, which is a direct result of colonisation. White thin women have been the paragon of beauty for so long that we turn a blind eye to the lack of cultural and ethnic diversity in the modelling and fashion industry. This is an attempt to assert dominance over marginalised women and is rooted in racism.

The pressure to conform to inconsistent and inclusive beauty standards has existed for centuries. But who decides what the beauty standard is? Well, if you look at some of the most successful fashion brands, it is men that are in charge. Givenchy, Versace, Gucci, Christian Louboutin, etc. When you look at the models in these early fashion shows, it is nobody's surprise that they are predominantly white thin women. While the selection of models has become slightly more progressive, the beauty standard still remains the same.

Understanding that the beauty standard is derived from racism, patriarchy and colonialism helps us break free from trying to conform to it. We have spent the majority of our lives trying to be something that we are not, and so it is time that we learn to accept who we are in our most authentic forms.

1. Why do you not feel beautiful in your natural body?

2. At what age do you remember first having bad body image thoughts?

_____

_____

_____

_____

_____

_____

_____

_____

3. How has social media affected your body image?

_____

_____

_____

_____

_____

_____

_____

_____

_____

_____

_____

_____

_____

4. Why do you place so much emphasis on the way your body looks?

_____

_____

_____

_____

_____

_____

_____

_____

5. How do you want to feel in your body?

_____

_____

_____

_____

_____

_____

_____

_____

_____

_____

_____

_____

_____

_____

_____

6. What makes you feel good about your body? If your answer is losing weight, why does losing weight make you feel better? Dive deep.

_____

_____

_____

_____

_____

_____

_____

_____

_____

_____

_____

_____

_____

_____

_____

_____

_____

_____

_____

_____

_____

_____

_____

_____

_____

Comparison

Eating disorders are very competitive in nature. We view everyone around us as threats, and that is difficult. How many times have you seen someone in public who is thin, and started judging yourself and comparing yourself to them? How many times have you gone out for food and someone else has ordered less than you, and that made you compare yourself to them? Competitiveness is a part of human nature, but it becomes unhealthy when comparison motivates us to do harmful things to ourselves and think harmful thoughts.

You have probably heard the phrase, 'comparison is the thief of joy', and that couldn't be more true. When you are comparing yourself to someone, you are perceiving them as a threat to you. Sometimes we are unaware of what we are competing for. Most of the time when it comes down to eating disorders, you are competing for the thinnest body and to be the sickest. But the harsh reality is that no matter how much weight you lose or how sick you deem yourself, there will always be someone else who you think is thinner and sicker. You can lose all the weight in the world, but there will always be someone who you compare yourself to and think that you are, in some way, losing.

Eating disorders thrive off competition. It is like fuel to a fire. Comparison is usually the reason we don't allow ourselves to recover, because we tell ourselves that we have to reach a level of sickness and thinness that we have seen others reach. But what if I told you that comparison never goes away?

That once you reach a level of sickness you once thought was *enough*, your eating disorder will disregard it and encourage you to get sicker?

Social media has allowed for comparison to thrive. There is a lot of content on social media that surrounds people's eating disorders, including photos of them in an unhealthy body, what they eat in a day, and discussions of dangerous behaviours. This opens up an opportunity for us to compare ourselves and think *well I never did that so I must not be valid or sick enough,* or *this person was in the hospital and I have never been.* In real life, it isn't normal to know every little detail about someone else and it is much easier to avoid knowing things that will ultimately lead to unhealthy comparisons. However, social media platforms like Instagram and TikTok trap us in a dome where it is incredibly difficult to avoid harmful content. And as much as it would be healthier for us to get off social media, it really is not that easy. We rely on social media for distraction and communication and we shouldn't have to sacrifice that because of the harmful and triggering content. While there aren't enough safety regulations in place to prevent us from seeing harmful content, there is not much we can do to change that.

If you have ever stumbled across the recovery community on social media, you will more often than not see a lot of content that encourages you to compare yourself. Even when you are recovering, there is almost a *right* way to recover displayed on social media, and if you do not conform, then it can make you feel invalid.

The issue with comparison is that it diverts your attention away from your own recovery journey, and focuses on other people and what and how they are recovering. I like to think of recovery as walking a tightrope.

Imagine you are on a tightrope. You start at the beginning which represents a time when you were actively engaging in your eating disorder, and the tightrope represents recovery. On the other end is life when you have recovered. To keep your balance on the tightrope, you shouldn't look back or around. You must look ahead. Now imagine there are hundreds and thousands of other people on their own tightrope. You are all lined up next to each other. If you are walking on a tightrope and begin to look around to see how far or head other people are doing, you will lose your balance, fall off the tightrope and have to start at the beginning again.

You have to stay focused on your own path, on your own journey and have tunnel vision. Keep looking forward, because the goal is to get to the other side. At times, you may feel scared of the other side. Maybe you are overwhelmed by how far left you have to cross until you get there, or maybe you are scared because you don't know what the view will look like from the other side. You might feel encouraged to turn around and walk back to the beginning, because you feel comfortable there. You have to have a lot of hope that the other side will be much better, and take it one step at a time. Keep looking forward, don't look around to see how everyone else is doing, and remember that the other side holds so much happiness. If you are focusing on what everyone else is doing, you are taking away the focus from your own path. You are recovering to get your life back, nobody else's. Your experience of an eating disorder will be different from everyone else's, and that is normal. Not everyone will have the same experience, and that doesn't take

away from your own. Other people's suffering is not the absence of your own.

Who are you recovering for?

At the beginning of recovery, you might feel that you don't want to recover, or that you want to go back into the arms of your eating disorder. Maybe you don't want to do it for yourself. This makes continuing difficult because you won't recover if you don't want to. You will eventually have to recover for yourself, but waiting for the day that you want to recover for yourself may delay the process.

The best thing you can do if this is your current situation is to decide to recover for something or someone. This could be family, or close friends, but I think the best reason to recover when you don't want to do it for yourself, is to do it for your younger self.

Imagine your younger self. They were small, young and naive to eating disorders. They didn't know what a calorie was, or that one day you would eventually end up battling an eating disorder. Maybe your younger self loved food and ate a lot of it. Imagine having a conversation with your younger self, and explaining to them what happened to you. Having to explain that you are battling a mental illness and that you no longer have a good relationship with food. Imagine how this would make your younger self feel.

1. Write a letter to your younger self about how things turned out

---

Don't be hard on yourself, you did not choose to have an eating disorder. But it can be helpful and motivating to keep your younger self in mind when recovering. Your younger self is you, and you are a grown-up version of that child. You both have all the same needs such as food, water, sleep, love, etc, but only now you don't fulfil your needs.

Find pictures of your younger self and show compassion to them. I bet it is easier to show compassion to that child than it is to yourself. But the ironic thing is that this child is you, and in ten years time, you will look back to who you are now and feel compassion. We keep that child within ourselves throughout our lives, and in the process of taking care of ourselves, we are ultimately taking care of that child.

Try and spend the day treating yourself the way you would treat your younger self if you could meet them again. Do all of the things they love, listen to their favourite music, take them to the park, etc. Whatever it is that your younger self loves, do that for a day. You are dedicating the day to your inner child. How does it make you feel to revisit your younger self? How do you imagine them reacting to who you have become? Remember, do not be hard on yourself. This is meant to spark compassion, not judgement.

1. Write down a conversation you would have with your younger self

_____

_____

_____

_____

_____

_____

_____

_____

_____

_____

_____

As I said, it is easier to have compassion for your younger self than it is to have compassion for yourself now.

1. Describe your relationship with food as a child

_____
_____
_____
_____
_____
_____
_____
_____
_____

How has your relationship with food changed?

_____
_____
_____
_____
_____
_____
_____
_____
_____

When you were a child, you most likely ate what you loved. You would get excited to eat your favourite foods, and you didn't care how eating those foods would impact your weight. You probably ate ice cream whenever you wanted and didn't think of the calories because you didn't know the calories.

If you could talk to your younger self, would you tell them about calories? Would you tell them to restrict so they didn't gain weight? I am guessing your answer is no. And if that is the case, then I want you to ask yourself why it is any different for you now.

If your younger self needed lots of food, then why do you think that you don't now? If a child needs lots of food, why doesn't an adult? An adult requires much more energy than a child, and yet you may believe that you don't deserve to eat as freely as you did as a child.

1. Why do you treat yourself any differently than how you would treat your younger self?

_____

_____

_____

_____

If you can, glue down a photo of your younger self on the next page. If not, change your lock screen photo to a photo of your younger self. Keep them in mind!

Now that you understand your eating disorder better, it will make recovery easy. When we understand something, it loses power over us because instead of us agreeing with the beliefs of our eating disorder, we can challenge them by rationalising them.

I like to think of eating disorders as having five stages. The first stage is the development of the disorder, which was the downward spiral, or drowning. The second stage is the depth of the eating disorder. Think of this as the bottom of the ocean. The third stage is acceptance, and this is like coming up for air. The fourth stage is recovery, where you swim back to shore. The final stage is recovered, and this is when you get back to shore. Identify which stage you are in. Maybe you are developing an eating disorder and want to educate yourself on how to stop it from spiralling any further, or maybe you are deep in your eating disorder. Maybe you are reading this book because you are at an important crossroads where you are not drowning, but not swimming either. You are floating above water wanting to swim to shore, but maybe you are being pulled back down to the bottom of the ocean. Maybe you are recovered and at the shore, but you still think it is necessary to educate yourself to help understand your disorder. Whatever stage you are in, it is important to identify your next steps.

Stage one: the drowning

At this point, you can recognise that you are spiralling deeper and deeper into an eating disorder. Maybe you have just started developing eating disorder behaviours and your thoughts are becoming increasingly about food. This is a conflicting stage because there is a part of you that wants to keep spiralling to see how bad things get. This is self-destruction and is talked about earlier on in the book. During this stage, you are drowning deeper into the water, and it is becoming increasingly more dangerous. The heavier the eating disorder, the more you are drowning and you don't know if you will ever stop.

It's common at this stage to find yourself comparing yourself to people who you consider worse than you, but it is important to know that you do **not** need to get worse before you can get better. You do not need to sink to the bottom of the ocean to be deserving of floating back up to the top. You are drowning regardless of how deep in you are. We often feel that we will only get taken seriously if we are as bad as we can get, and yet this is not true. However, if you have ever experienced professionals or loved ones invalidating your struggles, it feels like the only option is to get worse to *prove* that you are struggling.

If you have experienced this, you know all too well how painful it is for your struggles to be invalidated. Reaching out for help is often a very challenging thing to do, and it will only make you feel worse if you are not met with validation or care. Please know that you are not alone, and the invalidation you feel is not a reflection of how much you are struggling, but it is a reflection of the lack of understanding, training and compassion of the other person.

The people who are invalidating you, whether they are professionals or not, have probably never experienced an eating disorder. If someone has never experienced something, they won't be able to fully understand what it is like. No medical textbook could ever explain just how painful and debilitating an eating disorder is. This isn't an attempt to justify invalidation, but to help us understand that it is not an *us* problem, it is a *them* problem.

Only you know the details of your eating disorder and how it has affected you, and it is not anyone else's place to judge the severity of your struggles. Although it is difficult, do not let anyone who invalidates you win.

The urge to get worse before you can get better is like going to the emergency room with a broken ankle, being told it is *only* a broken ankle, and wanting to break your entire leg just so people take it seriously. But what good would that do? You would only be increasing your level of pain and the time it takes to heal, so is that really worth receiving a little more validation? You are in pain and that is enough suffering. You do not need to get worse before you begin to recover. You will have to recover eventually, so why postpone it? Why draw out your suffering if in the end, you will have to recover anyway?

You do not need to get worse before you get better, and yet you may feel like you have to.

1. Write down why you feel the urge to get worse before you get
    better?

Having an eating disorder is a struggle enough, you do not need to
experience every symptom or side effect for it to be considered a *real* eating
disorder. Maybe you are experiencing **imposter syndrome.**

Imposter syndrome is defined as feeling like a fraud. Maybe you doubt
whether you are sick enough, or maybe you doubt whether you have an
eating disorder at all. This is very common to experience with any mental
illness or disorder, but it can be stopped. Acceptance is the antidote to
imposter syndrome, so by working on accepting that the pain you suffer is
real and enough, you are overcoming the doubt that lingers surrounding the
existence of your eating disorder.

Stage two: the ocean floor

Maybe you feel like you are too far gone, that you couldn't possibly feel worse and your eating disorder has full control over you. If you are at this stage, you may feel like there is no way out.

Being in this stage of an eating disorder is terrifying because you feel like this is how your life will remain, that you will never overcome the eating disorder, and maybe you don't even want to. While this stage is absolutely terrifying, it can also be a comfort. This is most likely the stage where you feel most numb to anything other than your eating disorder, and maybe you perceive that to be a good thing. We usually develop eating disorders to numb pain, or to seek control in our lives. But the irony is, while we are trying to numb our pain and seek control, we are only creating new forms of pain and surrendering our control. Understanding that you are not in control is key to getting out of this trap.

Maybe this is the point where you are struggling the most mentally, or maybe even physically. Maybe your weight has dropped to the lowest it has been in a while, and while we know rationally that is not a good thing, our eating disorders will celebrate this and perceive it as a win.

Being at your lowest weight is nothing like how you probably imagined. You won't receive the confidence you thought you would, and maybe your body image is constantly fluctuating. Our eating disorders tell us that all the pain will be worth it when we are thin, but that couldn't be further from the truth.

If you have lost weight as a result of your eating disorder, you will probably feel euphoric for a few minutes, and then your eating disorder will decide that you need to lose more weight. You will never receive the satisfaction you think you will receive, and you will never feel that the weight you have lost is enough. Maybe you can't see yourself the way you truly are because body dysmorphia has plagued your self-perception. Your experience of being at your lowest weight won't be rainbows and sunshine like YOU are made to believe, it will most likely be an awful experience mentally and physically.

We know this, and yet we still believe the eating disorder every time it tells us that we will finally feel *sick enough* and confident if we lose more weight. How much more weight do you have to lose before you realise it will never be enough?

1. Why do you continue trying to please your eating disorder when you know it will never be enough?

----

2. Describe what *rock bottom* means to you?

_____

_____

_____

_____

_____

_____

_____

_____

_____

If you are at rock bottom, the good news is you have no further to fall. This is both a terrifying place to be and a transformative place to be. You have the opportunity to turn things around. What do you have to lose by trying to recover?

One of the best blessings in disguise for me personally was hitting rock bottom. It was an awful time and in no way does it deserve glamourising, but at the same time, it led me to realise that if I had nothing else to lose, why not try to recover? If it didn't work out and was as awful as my eating disorder was telling me it was, then I could always go back to how things were.

If you are in a situation where you feel like you are at rock bottom, try to do things differently. You have spiralled already and that obviously did not make anything better, so why not try something different? Why not try and spend at least a week being kind to yourself and going against the eating disorder thoughts? You have nothing to lose by trying to recover, so go for it.

This stage is like a leap of faith. You don't have much hope that things will work out well, but you also don't know for sure how things will turn out. Maybe this will be the best decision you ever made.

Nobody who fully recovers from an eating disorder regrets choosing recovery. The abundance and happiness that recovery brings overpowers your fear of weight gain and your fear of letting the eating disorder go. However, this mentality will take some time to get to. Recovery doesn't work overnight, which is why you have to trust the process and give recovery a real fair shot before you can make any conclusions about it. Start with one week. Do things differently and document your experience in this journal.

1. Note down what changes you are making and how they make you feel. Note down how you physically feel and any struggles you encounter. Note down any eating disorder thoughts you have and attempt to rationalise them. Remember, recovery takes time and you won't be feeling your best straight away.

The beginning is always the hardest. You will still have a lot of eating disorder thoughts and maybe you haven't been able to stray away from acting upon urges or behaviours. But don't give up yet. This is the hardest part and also the most fragile part. If you give up now, you won't get to the stage in recovery where everything feels easier and amazing changes are made. Recovery is a journey, and just like anything, starting is always the hardest part. You can do this, you have the strength within you to turn things around for the better, no matter how strong the eating disorder thoughts are. If you give up now, you will never get to feel and see the benefits that recovery has to offer.

If you are at rock bottom, you have nothing else to lose. Give recovery your best shot and see how things turn out. You can always go back if it is as dreadful as you believe it to be, but I promise with time, you will feel so glad that you chose recovery that you will never want to go back.

Stage three: coming up for air

If you are at a crossroad in your life where you are battling between choosing recovery and continuing to engage in your eating disorder, the key is maintenance until you figure it out.

Eating disorders are more complex than either being in or out of recovery. One thing nobody talks about is the middleground, where you are not fully in recovery but also not out of it. Maybe for now, all you can do is maintain your health and mental state. Maybe you are not trying to lose weight, but also not ready to commit to recovery and gain weight. For now, this is better than trying to lose weight and continuing to spiral deeper and deeper into your eating disorder. If all you can do is the bare minimum, that is enough. Making sure you are eating enough, resting enough and not having any goals surrounding weight gain/loss is okay, and this is a very transformative stage in your journey.

Maybe you don't feel ready to dive straight into recovery, it is terrifying and a big change so don't be hard on yourself. But here is a harsh reality I think is important to know. You will **never** feel ready to recover. You won't wake up and have a lightbulb moment where recovery feels like the right decision, it never will until you are further into your recovery journey. There isn't a right and a wrong time to recover, there is just a time to recover and it is right now. Don't be fooled and tell yourself that you're just not ready yet, because you will never feel ready to recover. Your eating disorder will always make you believe there is more weight to lose, more ways to self-destruct, more goals to reach, but that doesn't mean you should give them your time of day. You have to start recovering as soon as possible, even when it doesn't feel like the right time or when you don't feel like you are *sick enough*. You won't feel sick enough so don't wait around for the day you do before starting to recover. Recovery is an amazing and empowering journey that you will embark on, and it doesn't have a set criteria for who can recover or when. There is no rulebook stating you have to be at your worst to recover, or that you have to be a certain weight or have had a certain amount of experiences relating to the disorder.

So, you have a choice. To continue floating, to drown, or to swim back to shore and continue your life the way you were intended. Your purpose is not to suffer, your purpose is not to lose weight, your purpose is something much greater and is waiting for you to discover it on the other side of recovery.

Stage four: swimming back to shore

This stage is known as recovery. It is the journey between life deep in an eating disorder, and life without an eating disorder. It is an exhausting yet exhilarating journey that will lead you to discover who you are and what your purpose is.

Recovery is not linear. At times you will struggle more than at other times, but it is a journey you must embark on regardless. Recovery is fighting for your life, it is fighting for your health and your happiness. It is rediscovering everything about yourself and becoming a version of yourself you have never met. It is a beautiful process that is equally as hard, but it is a process that is worth every hard day. When you begin recovery, there are a lot of questions that you don't have the answer to, so the next section of this journal focuses on the process of recovery and the many twists and turns to expect.

Stage five: back at shore

This is the point where you consider yourself recovered. After all your hard work, you are no longer controlled by your eating disorder. It can be hard to imagine yourself at this stage, but it is possible. A full recovery from your eating disorder is entirely possible, and you won't spend the rest of your life controlled by thoughts of food and weight. We often believe that we will spend the rest of our lives being controlled by our eating disorders because when you are in the depths of one, it is hard to see any way out or imagine life any differently than how it already is. This mindset makes us lose hope that things get better, and often discourages us from even starting recovery because what is the point if you don't see anything changing? But the thing is, things will change. Nothing is permanent and your eating disorder doesn't have to be in control for the rest of your life. If you commit to recovery, you are getting closer and closer to being recovered and being able to live life for what it is meant to be, not what your eating disorder tells you it should be. Your purpose is far greater than losing weight and punishing yourself, and the journey of recovery will show you this. If nothing changes, then nothing will change. A cliché that we often hear, and yet it couldn't be more true. You have to break free from your destructive and unhealthy cycle to be able to experience life without your eating disorder.

Realising you need to recover

It can be difficult to realise how desperately you need to recover when you are still convinced you are not sick enough and that there is more you need to do to please your eating disorder. Your eating disorder doesn't have an end-point and it will never be satisfied, which is why so many people never make a full recovery. If you keep trying to please your eating disorder, you will always be trapped in a vicious cycle. You don't start recovery when you feel like you've lost enough weight or done enough awful things to your mind and body, because you will never feel like this. You will never feel like you have done *enough* to please your eating disorder or that you have lost *enough* weight. No, this won't happen, and postponing recovery until you feel this way just means you will never start recovery. Recovery has to be started as soon as possible, in spite of anything. You cannot wait to start recovery because the longer you push it off, the harder it will be to ever start and that is a deadly game to play.

You will never feel ready to recover, so you have to rely on feeling done with the eating disorder. Are you sick and tired of being controlled, of having no voice in your actions, of constantly being dominated by thoughts of food and weight? I understand how distressing this is. You have to use this anger and frustration as a catalyst for your recovery and jump into the deep end. But where do you start? How do you even begin to start recovering? It will be different for every individual, but there are some things you can do today that will push you in the right direction.

Stop your behaviours:

Whatever it is that your eating disorder encourages you to do, whether it is calorie count, weighing yourself, or any other behaviour, you have to stop. I have talked previously about how to stop these behaviours, so now you know, it is time to put this into practice. We often wait for a shift in our thoughts before making any changes, but this is not helpful in recovery. A change in your actions has to come first because it will take a while before you notice any mental changes. So, change your actions. Break out of the cycles and routines and do something different. Delete your calorie tracking apps, make yourself rest, and eat something different that your eating disorder doesn't consider 'safe'. Act differently to how your eating disorder wants you to act because this is how your thoughts will gradually change. Commit to challenging yourself today, in any way shape or form, as long as you are not listening to what your eating disorder wants.

How are you challenging yourself today?

_____

_____

_____

_____

_____

_____

_____

Why are you challenging yourself?

_____

_____

_____

_____

_____

_____

_____

_____

What will you do differently?

_____

_____

_____

_____

_____

_____

_____

How will you cope if it gets hard?

_____

_____

_____

_____

_____

_____

_____

How did the challenge go?

_____

_____

_____

_____

_____

_____

What did you observe yourself feeling?

_____

_____

_____

_____

_____

_____

How did you cope?

_____

_____

_____

_____

_____

_____

How did you feel afterwards?

_____

_____

_____

_____

_____

_____

How are you challenging yourself today?

_____

_____

_____

_____

_____

_____

_____

Why are you challenging yourself?

_____

_____

_____

_____

_____

_____

_____

_____

What will you do differently?

_____

_____

_____

_____

_____

_____

_____

How will you cope if it gets hard?

_____

_____

_____

_____

_____

_____

_____

_____

How did the challenge go?

_____

_____

_____

_____

_____

_____

What did you observe yourself feeling?

_____

_____

_____

_____

_____

_____

How did you cope?

_____

_____

_____

_____

_____

_____

_____

How did you feel afterwards?

_____

_____

_____

_____

_____

_____

_____

How are you challenging yourself today?

_____
_____
_____
_____
_____
_____

Why are you challenging yourself?

_____
_____
_____
_____
_____
_____
_____

What will you do differently?

_____
_____
_____
_____
_____
_____

How will you cope if it gets hard?

_____
_____
_____
_____
_____
_____

How did the challenge go?

_____

_____

_____

_____

_____

_____

_____

What did you observe yourself feeling?

_____

_____

_____

_____

_____

_____

_____

How did you cope?

_____

_____

_____

_____

_____

_____

_____

How did you feel afterwards?

_____

_____

_____

_____

_____

_____

_____

Don't panic if it didn't go swimmingly. The first few days, weeks and months in recovery are the hardest. Your thoughts will be overwhelmed by the eating disorder which may try to convince you that you are doing the wrong thing, that bad things will happen, and that you should feel guilty. But no matter how overpowering these thoughts are, remind yourself that you are doing the right thing, that you have done nothing wrong by challenging the eating disorder, and that you are in the process of getting your life back. What a wonderful thing!

Recovery is physically and mentally difficult, but it is important you remember how difficult and draining it was constantly trying to please and obey your eating disorder. People often say, 'choose your hard', when referring to recovery, but you have to remember that the difficulty of recovery doesn't last forever, while the difficulty of living in the depths of your eating disorder does last forever. So, yes, pick your battle, but remember that the battle of recovery is the fight to get your life back, and has a happy ending.

Dealing with triggers

In recovery, there will be many times when you feel triggered. This will open a flood of thoughts such as *I need to relapse, I need to lose weight,* etc. Learning how to deal with these triggers is crucial in recovery because they are inevitable. Social media makes it incredibly easy for us to be triggered. There is a lot of content out there which encourages disordered behaviours which is why you have to create distance between yourself and this content.

1. Go on your social media accounts and unfollow any accounts that are unhelpful. If you don't know how to identify these accounts, ask yourself how you feel after viewing their content. Do these accounts encourage disordered eating, promote diet culture, or post information about their own mental health that leaves you feeling invalid? If so, it is time to unfollow.

We don't realise that the content we see on social media affects us in profound ways. We may spend up to 10 hours a day scrolling on social media, and we are constantly seeing contradictory messages that challenge us. Maybe you follow some helpful recovery accounts, but occasionally see some triggering content from other accounts. This varied mix of content can cause you to feel confused, especially about whether you should continue recovering or not. Choosing recovery every day is hard enough as it is without the influence of social media, so go ahead and limit what type of content you can see so that it is helpful, and not unhealthy and damaging to your mental health.

Triggers don't all come from social media. Maybe your family or friends, or even professionals, have said something that has upset you. When we are in recovery, it is common for us to experience people telling us how much healthier we look, which to us, translates as 'you look fat'. While this can be very uncomfortable for us to hear, it is important we recognise that people do not mean harm by making these comments, because to them, this is a compliment. If you feel comfortable, explain to this person how comments of that nature can be very uncomfortable for you to hear, and that they should refrain from making any comments relating to your appearance. Remember, when they say *you look healthy*, it does NOT mean *you look fat*. That is your eating disorder attempting to allure you back into its arms by playing on your fear of weight gain.

Additionally, it isn't uncommon for people to talk about weight loss or dieting. Our society is very focused on losing weight and so it is difficult to avoid diet-related discussions. However, if you can, take yourself out of that environment and explain how you do not find discussion of diets and weight helpful to you. You should not be subjected to these discussions during your recovery. If these discussions do trigger you, remind yourself that it has nothing to do with you. You do **not** need to lose weight or partake in **any** weight-loss activity or diet. You are on your own path, your own journey, and weight loss has absolutely no place in it.

If you struggled with body-checking, specifically taking photos of your body, I urge you to delete the photos. Seeing photos of your body when you were in the depths of an eating disorder won't help you, but it will deter you away from gaining weight (which is necessary). By having a constant reminder of what you used to look like, you are stopping yourself from moving forward and growing into the better version of yourself - one that is healthy and happy. Keep in mind that a *healthy* body does not relate to BMI at all. Your healthy body is what you have when you are not engaging in eating disorder behaviours or restricting or compensating in any way shape or form.

Weight restoration

In recovery from restrictive eating disorders, it means you need to restore your weight. But what exactly does that mean? This does not mean reaching what the Body Mass Index (BMI) spectrum refers to as healthy, this is individual and different for everyone. Weight restoration involves restoring the weight you lost, but isn't limited to this. It is about finding your set point weight, which will fluctuate over years and is different for everyone.

If you lost weight from an eating disorder, no matter how much or little, you will need to gain that back. But why? Why can't you just stay the size you are? Well, telling yourself that you can recover from a restrictive eating disorder without weight restoration is like saying you can cook a cake without an oven. Weight restoration is one of many key parts of recovery, and you cannot avoid it while claiming to be recovering. If you restricted your food intake as a result of your eating disorder, weight restoration will have to occur during your recovery to ensure you are recovering. If you listen to your eating disorder and it is telling you that you can maintain your weight and avoid gaining in recovery, then you are not truly recovering. Recovery from an eating disorder vaguely means overcoming whatever fears exist, and if weight gain is one of your fears, then you can understand why not avoiding it is key.
Just like getting over a fear of heights entails exposing yourself to heights, overcoming your fear of weight gain entails exposing yourself to weight gain.

You may be telling yourself that this doesn't apply to you, that you don't need to gain any weight, but ask yourself what you would say to someone else in the same position as you. If you were standing in front of someone who has struggled with an eating disorder, would you tell them that they do not need to weight restore? I am guessing you wouldn't, and maybe you would tell them how important it is to restore their weight. Now envision the person you are talking to as you. Pretend to be someone else just for a moment. What advice would you tell yourself?

Gaining weight can be very daunting, but it does get easier. The more weight you gain, the less scary it becomes because each time you gain, you know how to cope and feel because you have done it before. But what happens if it doesn't get easier? What happens when you feel the urge to relapse and lose weight?

Relapse vs Recovery

This is a very difficult position to be in. You have one part of you that is telling you to keep going, and you have the eating disorder within you telling you to relapse and lose weight. You are stuck between the two, divided and struggling to commit to either one. This is a cycle that a lot of us find ourselves caught up in. The cycle consists of recovery and relapse, and throughout your life, maybe you have been going between the two, but never found a way out. Life doesn't solely consist of recovering and relapsing over and over, in fact, you won't be recovering forever, but that doesn't mean relapsing is the alternative. Living your life having recovered from your eating disorder is entirely possible, and is the destination of your recovery journey.

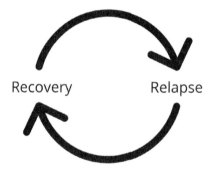

Recovery   Relapse

This is probably what your current cycle looks like.

Recovery ⟶ Recovered

This is what we wish recovery was.

This is what recovery will most likely be like. A constant up-and-down journey. Sometimes it will feel easier than other times, and sometimes it will feel so difficult you think you are going backwards. Remember that recovery is not linear, each day will be different, and it is okay if you have taken a step back, as long as you are continuing in the right direction. You are not perfect, and at times you may feel challenged and made to feel like the easier option is to relapse, but I promise you that you have not come this far to only go this far. You have worked so hard and you are strong enough to fight the urges to relapse. Just keep reminding yourself why you are recovering, and why you are fighting so hard. You have got this.

1. Write down why you should fight the urge to relapse

Do you ever feel like you have unfinished business with your eating disorder? Do you ever feel like there is further to fall? More weight to lose, more ways to hurt yourself, and new levels of sickness to achieve. If you feel like this, you are not alone. In fact, a big reason why so many of us delay recovery is because we do not feel like we have finished, as if we have duties to carry out and goals to reach to please our eating disorder. Maybe you feel like it isn't the right time to recover, but I am here to tell you that there is no right or wrong time to recover. The time is now. If you are postponing recovery, you are ultimately postponing the inevitable, so why wait? You know deep down that you will have to recover at some point in your life, so why wait another year? You won't grow out of an eating disorder, it needs to be tackled head-on as soon as possible to prevent it from affecting your life any further. The longer you postpone recovery, the more time you are wasting to put it bluntly. You have a life to live, a beautiful life waiting for you (even if you cannot see it right now), and your eating disorder is robbing you of that. It is a thief, a bully, and it is not serving you. Your eating disorder wants you to be sick, to be miserable, lost, and trapped, and it has no good intention for you. Whatever unfinished business you think you have with it, recognise that this is just your eating disorder's attempt to maintain power over you. Yes, there will always be more weight to lose, but at what cost? How much longer will you surrender your control to your eating disorder and allow it to take everything good away from you? You did not choose to develop an eating disorder, but you have the choice, you have the **power** to choose recovery. Do not postpone it any longer. You have already spent enough time hurting yourself by listening to it. Life won't wait for you, it will pass you by unless you choose to recover and reclaim your life back. People will grow up, get jobs, graduate, and find love, and that is not going to be easy to see if you are still

117

stuck in your eating disorder. You could be growing up, moving on, and finding your purpose, but you can't do that if you are still trapped. Break free. I dare you. You have the strength, you have the choice, and you have to power. Choose to recover.

1. What is holding you back?

_____

_____

_____

_____

_____

_____

_____

_____

_____

_____

_____

_____

_____

_____

_____

_____

_____

_____

_____

Recovery feels like failure

I have spoken previously about **imposter syndrome,** and this connects to feelings of failure in and out of recovery. It seems that our eating disorders set us up for failure from the get-go. No matter how much weight you lose, how much control you surrender to your eating disorder, or how much time and thought you give to it, it is never enough. This will lead to you feeling like a failure because you will never be able to fully satisfy your eating disorder or accomplish all the disordered goals it wants you to. Maybe you feel ready to recover because you are tired of feeling like a failure, but the bad news is that feelings of failure do not disappear when you enter recovery. In fact, it is common that these feelings worsen the more you go against the eating disorder, and so it makes recovery even more difficult to continue. If you are going against the eating disorder voice, you are most likely going to experience strong thoughts of failure because you are not letting it control you. This is a good thing, and yet it can feel very wrong. Maybe you are experiencing guilt and negative thoughts about yourself, or maybe your eating disorder is telling you that you have failed.

I want you to know that you are not alone. It is very common to experience these horrible feelings in recovery, but it is important to know that they do go away. Recovery is never a failure, in fact, recovery is a success. You are succeeding and winning your life back by choosing to recover, even when it feels like the opposite. Recovery brings about lots of negative feelings such as guilt, failure, feeling like a fraud, and so on. But these feelings eventually subside. However, it might be that you feel the urge to relapse just to lessen the impact of these thoughts and to stop feeling such negative emotions

119

towards yourself and your life. This is a temporary fix because while acting on urges may release negative emotions for a bit, they will end up coming back in full force. To completely eradicate these feelings of guilt and failure, you will have to expose yourself to them over and over. This is what makes recovery so draining. You have to constantly push yourself to challenge these eating disorder thoughts and resist acting upon urges. The more you expose and challenge yourself, the less powerful these thoughts and feelings become, and eventually, they won't even be there. If you are feeling the force of these awful thoughts right now, I want you to know that they do go, but only if you continue acting against your eating disorder.

Even though feelings of guilt and failure encourage us to run back to our eating disorders, I want you to think of these negative emotions as a source of motivation to recover. This is why you are recovering in the first place - to get rid of these negative feelings and thoughts. Instead of considering relapsing, try to reframe your thoughts and use this as fuel for your recovery. Tell yourself *I want to recover so I no longer feel these negative emotions towards myself or my life. I am recovering because I want to live my life and have a healthy relationship with food, and yes, these negative thoughts will come, but they will also pass.* The thoughts always pass.

Recovery is not failure. Weight gain is not failure. In fact, you are succeeding if you are managing to go against your eating disorder. You are doing the best thing for yourself by recovering, even when it doesn't feel like it.

Why do we feel like failures?

There is a part of us that believes our eating disorders are something to accomplish. Think of all the goals your eating disorder has pushed you towards, or why you feel competitive against other eating disorder sufferers. The nature of an eating disorder is competitive, and it almost feels like we are in a race and the end goal is achieving the ultimate level of sickness. If we see everyone with an eating disorder as competitors in this race, it makes it easier to understand why we view others as competition. If you are feeling triggered by someone, it may be that you view them as *ahead* of you in this race. Maybe you believe they are sicker than you, and in this analogy, that means they are closer to the finish line. But take a step back and ask yourself what this race is. This race is run by sick people trying to beat other sick people, and show *who has it worse,* and *who is most sick.* But the thing is, it isn't a good thing to win this race. Yes, it may fill you with feelings of achievement, but really, you are competing in a race that will only end in illness and death. You are running away from your life and running towards your death.

The Eating Disorder Race

Life ·······························> Death

We often tell ourselves that our eating disorders are not *that bad*, that we will be fine, and that we are the exception to the statistics. We often believe that we will be fine, that we are not sick enough for this illness to have any health complications that result in death, but that is not true. You can die as a result of an eating disorder at any weight, and you are not the exception. It could be you. I do not say this to scare you, but at the same time, it is important we understand the fatal nature of this deadly illness. It is something we should be scared of because the possibility of death is not fictional. It does happen, and many people have died as a result of an eating disorder.

The National Association of Anorexia Nervosa and Associated Disorders (ANAD) reported that 5-10% of anorexics die within 10 years of contracting the disease and that 18-20% of anorexics will be dead after 20 years. The mortality rate associated with anorexia nervosa is 12 times higher than the death rate of ALL causes of death for females aged 15-24 years old.Bulimia is shown to double the risk of premature death and has an estimated mortality rate of 4%. ED-NOS is estimated to have a mortality rate of around 5.2%. Additionally, the suicide rates were found to be very high. Suicide attempts were estimated at around 31.4% for sufferers of bulimia, 22.9% for those who suffer from binge eating disorders, and 24.9% for anorexic sufferers. These rates are extremely high and highlight just how fatal eating disorders are, whether sufferers die from physical health complications or suicide. You are not the exception, and if you suffer from an eating disorder, you have a heightened risk of premature death. This is what makes recovery so much more necessary. You are saving your own life by choosing to recover, and you do not have time to push recovery back until you feel ready.

But what happens if you are also struggling with suicidal thoughts? If you are experiencing depression or/and suicidal thoughts, recovery becomes that much harder. Maybe you believe that there is no point fighting for your life if you do not want to live it. If you are struggling, I urge you to reach out and seek professional support because there are people who want to help you and keep you safe. From my personal experience, I used my eating disorder to numb my suicidal thoughts, and yet at the same time, the worse my eating disorder became, the worse the suicidal thoughts were. Eating disorders make us lose hope and make us believe that we will only ever feel good if we lose weight or seek control. Ask yourself whether your eating disorder makes you feel genuinely good. Eating disorders numb us from our pain and give us something to focus on that isn't what we are trying to avoid, but at the same time, eating disorders create a whole new group of issues. It seems to be that, more often than not, we engage in self-destructive coping mechanisms to lessen the pain, by creating a different and new experience of pain. Pain begets pain. When you are feeling hopeless and feeling like you will never be happy, it is important to know that things are temporary. Things change so fast, and even though change is daunting, it is also important and comforting because it provides us with the understanding that no matter how bad we feel, we won't feel it forever. If you are dealing with suicidal thoughts, you know just how well how difficult they make recovery. If you don't see a positive future ahead of you, it makes it difficult to *try* to get better. Think about it this way instead. If you are at rock bottom, you have nothing to lose by trying to get better. One thing I always found helpful was telling myself that I could always go back if recovery really was all that terrible, but it wasn't terrible at all, in fact, recovery was the best decision I ever made. So, if you think this will help, tell yourself that you can always go back if things don't improve, but that you also have nothing to lose by truly giving recovery your best shot. I guarantee if you view recovery in this way (that you have nothing to lose and everything to gain), then it becomes easier. Hope trickles in slowly in recovery, and before you know it, you will regain your contentment and happiness.

You have nothing to lose and everything to gain.
You have nothing to lose and everything to gain.
You have nothing to lose and everything to gain.
You have nothing to lose and everything to gain.

How to start fearing your eating disorder and not recovery

When you are deep in your eating disorder, you may find that recovery is a very daunting and scary concept. We seek comfort in our eating disorders and we become trapped in routines and cycles. Our eating disorder becomes our new normal, so we stop fearing the consequences and the detrimental and fatal nature of the illness. But it is important to attempt to redirect your fear. Fear protects us from things we perceive to be a danger, but when you fear recovery, you start believing that recovery is a threat and not your actual eating disorder.

Eating disorders are often glamorised on social media which contributes to the fear of recovery and the indulgence of the illness. It is important we educate ourselves on the dangers of this illness so we can see it for what it truly is. Many studies have highlighted just how dangerous eating disorders are, and just how big of a toll they take on our bodies.

Decreased red blood cell count   Electrolyte imbalance

Infertility   Increased risk of heart failure

Hypothermia

Dry skin   Gastroparesis

Osteopenia

Severe bloating   Bacterial infections

Death

Unstable blood sugar levels   Anemia   Osteoporosis

.   Hair loss
Insulin resistant   Constipation

Brittle hair
Damaged nerve endings in intestines

Ruptured stomach

Ruptured oesophagus

Pancreatitis

Intestinal obstructions   Kidney failure

Lowered sex hormones

Reduced metabolic rate   High cholestrol levels

Extreme Hunger: Is it Normal?

Recovery would be much easier if we could go from restricting to magically eating a "normal" amount of food. However, this isn't always the case. Often, we underestimate the amount of food we need in recovery, and also may experience something known as *extreme hunger*.

Extreme hunger refers to the intensified desire to eat and is a natural bodily response to a period of restriction. When your body has been through a period of starvation and recognises that you can eat food abundantly, it reacts by driving you to eat amounts of food you may not feel comfortable eating. It is almost as if your body is screaming out for food, even if you feel physically full. Mental hunger and physical hunger are different but equally as important. Mental hunger looks like constantly thinking of food, wanting to eat more, and never feeling mentally satisfied by how much or what you are eating. Physical hunger is physically feeling hunger in your stomach, maybe feeling weak and lightheaded, or maybe you have eaten but feel a physical need to eat more. It is important to understand that these types of hunger are different in the sense that you could be physically full and mentally hungry.

It is already difficult to understand your hunger cues in recovery because they will have been thrown off by the period of restriction. It is hard to know when to eat if you have been ignoring your hunger signals for so long. To overcome this and to regulate your hunger signals, it might be helpful to set yourself the goal of having your 3 meals, and 3 snacks at set times. Do not worry if you are late or early when you eat, and definitely do not panic if you have more

127

food than 3 meals and 3 snacks, this is just a **minimum** in recovery, but it should help you regulate your hunger cues by eating even when you do not necessarily want to.

I bet there have been times during the depths of your eating disorder when all you would fantasise about was consuming large amounts of food. Well, the good news about extreme hunger is that you can finally honour all your cravings and satisfy your hunger. There is nothing wrong or bad about extreme hunger, in fact, it is a good sign that you are heading in the right direction. You may feel overwhelmed by how strong your hunger is, but do not panic. Although this is known as *extreme* hunger, there is absolutely nothing extreme about it. In fact, you cannot expect your body to go through periods of restriction and then just resume as normal. As I explained in the oxygen analogy, your body is in an energy deficit and will need to *pay off* the debt. Honour your cravings, whatever they are, and let your body and mind heal. Remember that no food is bad or good, that food simply does not have any moral value, and that you are doing the right thing by honouring your hunger.

Extreme hunger is terrifying because you have gone from one extreme to another, but remind yourself that this is a normal and natural bodily response to a period of starvation and is required.

Tabitha Farrar came up with a great analogy to explain extreme hunger. If you owed someone £1,000,000 and only ever gave them £1000 every now and then, they would be constantly asking for more money. This is the same with energy. If your body requires a certain amount of energy and you have not been giving it over time, the energy deficit builds up and your body will be screaming out for more energy. Give your body the energy it asks for. Extreme hunger is merely the process of restoring your energy and allowing your body to heal. Extreme hunger is not wrong or bad, and it definitely is nothing to feel ashamed about. You are not alone. Your body is going through a very vital stage of healing.

Will extreme hunger ever stop? Yes, however, it is important that you do not think of it this way. You won't wake up one day and be able to eat like a *normal* person. It takes time and some days your hunger will be more intense than on other days. Honour it every day, to whatever extent, and know that this is part of the recovery process.

1. Why are you scared to truly honour your hunger?

2. What will happen if you honour your hunger?

_____

_____

_____

_____

_____

_____

_____

_____

_____

_____

_____

_____

_____

_____

_____

_____

_____

_____

_____

_____

_____

_____

_____

_____

_____

_____

Things I wish I knew before recovery

1. People won't love you less if you recover

A big fear of mine was that everyone would stop caring about me if I got better, and that nobody would support me if I no longer *looked* unwell. This was a huge obstacle standing in the way of me and weight gain. As I gained the weight back, I realised that people were actually more happy to be around me. When you recover and gain weight, you have the mental capacity to care about things besides food and weight. You will get your hobbies back, your passions, and you will become a nicer person to be around. People enjoy your presence more in recovery because you are regaining your personality, and that is far more special to people who love you than them seeing you suffer. They won't stop caring either. You will be surprised by how supportive people are, and remember that the people who love you want you to get better. Nobody wants you to be sick, it is hard for people to see someone they love sick because they feel helpless. Keep people close, and rely on them as your support system throughout your recovery because you do not have to go through this alone. Reach out to people and do not be afraid to ask them for some motivation or reassurance. A good support system is crucial in recovery from any illness, mental or physical.

2. Life in a bigger body is not bad

One of the fears we have is weight gain. The thought of gaining weight is terrifying for all sorts of reasons. I always believed that things would get worse if I restored my weight and that I wouldn't be able to handle it mentally. However, the more weight I gained, the happier I became and the bigger my life became. I gained the energy to do exciting things, I began to feel more comfortable in my body, my sleeping improved, and a lot of the horrible symptoms of my eating disorder subsided. My body felt warm, safe, and more energised than ever. I never wanted to admit this, but even when I hated my body, my eating disorder told me I looked better than I did at a healthy weight. I used to think I would have a worse body if I gained weight, that I would no longer like my body at a higher weight and that I was generally prettier when I looked unwell. This mentality stayed with me for a while in my early recovery, and that is understandable because often, physical changes happen before mental changes. I used to fear that my mind would still be unwell but I would be trapped in a bigger body, so nobody would take me seriously. Because as hard as these things are to admit, it is important to acknowledge your disordered thoughts **as** disordered. These thoughts are very common for people with eating disorders, and I want to tell you something that I wish someone told me. The fear you have of weight gain and your reasons for being afraid are rooted in shame. The shame you felt for your body before you lost any weight may be the reason you are so scared to be that weight or more again. In my life, I have been on both ends of the spectrum and I remember the misery I felt every time I looked in the mirror. I associated that misery with what I saw in the mirror, and thought if I could change what I saw, I would no longer feel misery. When I lost weight, I would look in the mirror and expect to feel differently, but no matter how much weight I lost, the feelings of misery never went away. It took me years of mental torture to discover that I couldn't change my feelings by changing my body. The issue was never what I saw in the mirror, the issue was the feeling. Now I realise that I never needed to change my body, I needed to change my thoughts and my habits of thinking. It was never my body, it was my mind, and that is when I accepted that no matter how much weight I lost, I would never feel any differently unless I changed my thoughts. So really, there is never a point in changing and manipulating the shape and size of your body, because that has no effect on the way you think. You can't induce a shift in your emotions by a shift in your physical body, your vessel.

3. Nobody wants you to be sick

One thing I always believed was that people around me, family, friends, doctors, and therapists, all wanted me to be sick. I used to go to my therapy sessions and treat weekly weigh-ins as a weight loss competition. I believe a part of my illness was believing that people wanted me to be sick and that it was my role to play the anorexic. However, now I have finally stopped therapy and can look back with the knowledge and wisdom I have now, I can see just how wrong I was. Nobody wanted me sick. Doctors weren't impressed when I lost weight, and my family was never judging how much I ate. In recovery, your relationships become so much better and you are finally able to acknowledge that the people around you only ever wanted you to get better. People who love you lose a sense of you when you are sick, and it may make people develop feelings of helplessness and frustration. People who love you may feel frustrated because they don't agree with the way you treat yourself, and it is never pleasant to watch someone you love be hurt, whether it is by themselves or another. The people around me weren't interested in my weight, the doctors only needed to weigh me to monitor me. I look back with clarity and correct all the irrational thoughts my eating disorder produced. I feel a lot of empathy for the people around me, and I even used to feel guilty, for thinking they wished sickness on me. I feel regret for how I treated the people around me, and one of the great things about recovery is that I am able to make positive memories involving food around the people I love. It almost feels like I am swapping all the bad memories I have and replacing them with happier, healthier memories. Nobody wanted me sick, nobody wanted me to lose weight. These were all disordered thoughts that held me back from choosing the right treatment path and not participating in therapy the way I should have. I feel a lot of regrets but I cannot change the past, so I am learning to accept and focus on creating lots of happy memories with the people I love.

4.   Weight gain gets less scary

Before I began my recovery journey, I was terrified of gaining weight. So, when I started recovery and gained weight, stepping on those scales felt awful. I believed that my body had punished me by making me gain weight because I didn't listen to my eating disorder. I used to view weight gain as a punishment for not doing "well" enough at losing weight that week, so this is generally how the first few weeks of weight gain went for me. The initial weight gain was terrifying, because I still was in the early stages of recovery and hadn't yet detached my worth from my weight. At this stage, I didn't think I would ever overcome the fear, but with repeated exposure to gaining weight, and with my improving mental health as a result of recovery, weight gain became less scary. I wish I knew that weight gain gets less scary before I started recovery, and even in the early stages of it. The further into recovery you are, the better your quality of life becomes and you get your love of life back, so weight gain seems so insignificant in comparison. The more full and abundant your life becomes in recovery, the less important things you used to deem important get. Recovery gave me my quality of life back and I know that if I ever relapsed or had a serious wobble in my recovery, I would have to sacrifice everything that now makes me happy and makes my life more abundant. Weight gain becomes increasingly insignificant the further you are in your recovery, so don't lose hope and believe that your fear of weight gain will always be there.

5. Food is just food

For years, food became this thing I loved but feared so greatly. Every aspect of my day revolved around food, and it was all I could think about. I used to fantasise about all the different food I would eat one day if I chose recovery, and yet, the fantasy slowly became a reality. When I think of my days in early recovery, food had so much flavour and every bite was sensational. The food was delicious and I couldn't get over how tasty it was. But at the same time, it was also scary. So at this point, food both excited and scared me, and so that made eating a big deal. But looking back in retrospect, food hasn't excited me recently the same way it used to. And why? Because the exaggerated reaction to food was just a reaction from years of bland and horrible food, as well as starvation. Yes, the food tasted good, but in my head, it felt like this huge deal. Throughout recovery, food has become less exciting and scary and has become just food. I now see food as this delicious source of energy that I need a lot of throughout each day. It isn't a big deal to me anymore, and food has become just food. Not a dictator of my worth, and not something that needs earning, but just food. A source of energy that also tastes good! I wish I could go back in time and tell myself that food is just food, it isn't good or bad, it isn't to be earned, and it isn't as big a deal as I thought it was. Food becomes just food, and that is wonderful because it means you are detaching your worth and seeing it for what it is; an important and delicious source of energy.

So… How much should you eat?

If you do not have access to a therapist, dietician, or any other form of professional help, then it can be very tricky to know how to start recovery from a nutritional perspective. It isn't as easy as telling you to eat a certain amount to recover because everyone who has an eating disorder needs a different individualised recovery plan. So, how do you know how much to eat or what you should eat? Firstly, It is very important that you seek medical help if you develop signs of refeeding syndrome (caused by rapid refeeding after a period of under-nutrition), so be cautious and look out for the signs:

- fatigue
- weakness
- confusion
- difficulty breathing
- high blood pressure
- seizures
- irregular heartbeat
- heart failure
- confusion

Now, where we begin our recovery from a nutritional standpoint will differ between us all but remember that the aim is to increase our intake and begin to incorporate foods we may have restricted, as well as challenge ourselves while building up our strength. This may sound terrifying, so take it one meal at a time. It can be very overwhelming so hopefully, this plan will help you.

1. Write down your current aims in terms of eating (e.g. foods you want to try, the number of meals you want to eat, etc). Think about now. What is your next step?

_____

_____

_____

_____

_____

_____

_____

_____

It can often help to write down a list of your fear foods if you have any, and tick them off throughout your recovery to document your progress and motivate you!

Foods I Want To Try

Today I will challenge my eating disorder by:

_____

_____

_____

_____

_____

_____

_____

Daily Overview

Did I manage my daily goal?   Yes ☐ No ☐

Reflect:

_____

_____

_____

_____

_____

_____

_____

_____

_____

*date :*_____

Today I will challenge my eating disorder by:

_____

_____

_____

_____

_____

_____

_____

_____

Daily Overview

Did I manage my daily goal?   Yes ☐ No ☐

Reflect:

_____

_____

_____

_____

_____

_____

_____

_____

_____

_____

_____

Today I will challenge my eating disorder by:

_____

_____

_____

_____

_____

_____

_____

_____

Daily Overview

Did I manage my daily goal?   Yes ☐ No ☐

Reflect:

_____

_____

_____

_____

_____

_____

_____

_____

_____

date:_____

Today I will challenge my eating disorder by:

_____

_____

_____

_____

_____

_____

_____

Daily Overview

Did I manage my daily goal?   Yes ☐ No ☐

Reflect:

_____

_____

_____

_____

_____

_____

_____

_____

_____

_____

Today I will challenge my eating disorder by:

_____

_____

_____

_____

_____

_____

_____

Daily Overview

Did I manage my daily goal?   Yes ☐ No ☐

Reflect:

_____

_____

_____

_____

_____

_____

_____

_____

_____

_____

_____

Today I will challenge my eating disorder by:

_____

_____

_____

_____

_____

_____

_____

_____

Daily Overview

Did I manage my daily goal?   Yes ☐ No ☐

Reflect:

_____

_____

_____

_____

_____

_____

_____

_____

_____

_____

_____

Today I will challenge my eating disorder by:

_____

_____

_____

_____

_____

_____

_____

_____

Daily Overview

Did I manage my daily goal?   Yes ☐ No ☐

Reflect:

_____

_____

_____

_____

_____

_____

_____

_____

_____

_____

Don't push it off

At many times you may find yourself questioning if you are ready for recovery. Maybe you don't feel ready to try foods that scare you or challenge your eating disorder at all. These feelings are very common, but just because you don't feel ready, it doesn't mean you're not. Nobody feels ready 100 percent of the time, but it doesn't mean you shouldn't challenge yourself. In fact, the feelings of unreadiness and nervousness surrounding the act of challenging your eating disorder is quite literally the reason why you should challenge it. It has power over you, and it is time to reclaim that power and get your life back. If you keep pushing off challenges and convincing yourself and others that you are not ready, you are only making it harder for yourself because ultimately you are giving the fear power and this means that the next time you try to challenge yourself, it will be harder.

Postponing recovery is no good. Nothing you do between now and committing to recovery is going to be worth the time and effort. Imagine you are sinking underwater. You are only making it harder for yourself if you decide to drown a little more before you swim back up for air. It doesn't matter if you are 5ft underwater or 20 ft under, you are still in danger and you are in need of help. So don't push off recovery any longer, the time to get better is now.

"I'm not thin enough to recover"

Being thin is not part of the diagnostic criteria for an eating disorder. And yet, we seem to tie our weight to our validity. And although we may be aware that our weight doesn't equate to how sick we are, we still adopt the belief that we are not thin enough to recover. So what does that actually mean?

One thing that isn't spoken about is how often your eating disorder thoughts go against your moral values. You may believe that weight doesn't determine someone's worth, and yet I bet your eating disorder has made you think otherwise when it comes to your own weight. If this is true, then It is likely that at some point you have told yourself that you're not thin enough to seek help, to be taken seriously, or to recover, and yet I bet that at some point you have told someone that they're valid no matter what they weigh. This double standard is very common when it comes to eating disorders, but it definitely needs addressing and overcoming. You have to learn how to apply the same rules that you apply to others, to yourself. Yes, this means disconnecting your own weight from your worth, as well as detaching your weight from your perception of your sickness. This looks like accepting that your weight is not an indicator of your sickness and that your weight does not play a role in deciding whether you deserve to get better or not. Recovery isn't earned. You don't earn the right to get better by getting as bad as you possibly can. And like I have previously said, you don't need to get worse before you get better.

The number on the scales does not determine just how bad your eating disorder is, but it is your mental suffering that determines the severity of your eating disorder. If you have suffered from a preoccupation with food, a disordered relationship with your diet and body whether that manifests physically or not, then you are in need of getting better and making a full recovery.

Eating disorders often make us think and do some very extreme and bizarre things, and maybe one of the disordered things your eating disorder has made you believe is that you have to get to the lowest possible weight before getting better, because then you "deserve" to get better. This serves as a justification as if your recovery needs to be earned through extreme weight loss. However, it doesn't. It doesn't need to be earned and you do not have to justify getting better to anyone, especially yourself. You will always have the power to get better, no matter what. That is something your eating disorder can never take away from you, even when it feels like it already has.

Social media doesn't need to see your bodychecks

Have you ever felt like you have had to prove your illness? Maybe you want to show people how much weight you have lost or show them how sick you are. This is actually very common in the recovery community on social media. A lot of recovery-focused accounts have been involved in uploading photos/videos or discussing the in-depth details of their illness and/or treatment, and this never receives positive feedback. It is common for sufferers of eating disorders to feel the need to validate their illness, and some do this by posting content that is often perceived as negative and comes off as triggering. If you have ever done this, then it is important to remember that it is irresponsible to validate yourself while simultaneously triggering others. Of course, not every post that people find triggering was posted with ill intentions, but we all personally have the responsibility to reduce the preexisting stigma and not contribute to stereotypes, while also ensuring we are not posting content that could trigger others. Keep in mind that you do not need external validation to be valid, and that validation is only important when it is internal. There is no good having hundreds of people validate your illness if you are not going to validate it yourself. And it most definitely is no good to attempt to validate your eating disorder by triggering others. Don't be hard on yourself if you have been in this position, everyone makes mistakes and all you can do is learn and commit to doing better. Social media is full of content that has the intention of worsening eating disorders, the last thing any of us need is that negative pro-eating disorder content filtering through into the recovery community. So, make it easier for yourself and

151

disengage from any content that doesn't motivate you, but worsens you. You can do this by blocking and reporting accounts, or simply unfollowing them. Similarly, if you are making content that can be interpreted as encouraging or glamorising disordered behaviours and habits, then take a step back and reevaluate whether social media is where you should be focusing your attention.

Is social media hindering your recovery?

There are communities for everything these days, and two of the most relevant communities are the pro-eating disorder and recovery communities. The pro-eating disorder community is also known as 'edtwt', 'edtumblr', 'pro-ana', 'pro-mia' and many other nicknames, and it has spread to every social media platform. You will even find this community on apps aimed at kids such as TikTok. These communities are known for promoting eating disorders as well as glamourise them. But if they are so problematic, then why are they so popular?

A lot of people struggling with an eating disorder want to have a space where they feel comfortable sharing their thoughts and details of their eating disorder including their weight, BMI, calorie intake, etc. It doesn't take long to find these communities on social media and be affected by what they encourage. There is very little protection in regards to coming across this type of negative content, and it can even be shown to us without us searching for it (for you pages on TikTok, etc). This content is extremely toxic and it has the potential to cause someone to develop an eating disorder, to keep pursuing their eating disorder, to relapse, and even to die. If you are familiar with these communities, then this applies to you. Maybe it provides you with a sense of comfort in having a place to turn to when you are struggling, but this type of content has no place in your recovery, and you have to get out of these communities as soon as possible. It is awful that these communities still exist on social media and that there isn't more being done by site managers to remove them, so you have to take responsibility yourself and know that if you are participating, delete your account. There is no room for sugar-coating when these corners of the internet have such huge potential to destroy people's mental health and even take lives. Delete your account and try your best to not revisit these sites, even when you feel the urge to trigger yourself.

So where else can you go to feel understood? As well as there being pro-eating disorder communities, there are also pro-recovery communities, and more often than not, these communities are safe spaces for you to feel understood and know that you are not alone. However, the recovery communities are not always going to leave you feeling motivated. Sometimes, you may come across some content that triggers you. The content that gets uploaded and remains on social media is not regulated as well as it should be, and so it is up to us as individuals to ensure that we are not contributing any negative or potentially triggering content.

It's become very common for people to share triggering content in the recovery community. These things may include bodychecks, details of their weight/BMI or treatment plan. While this may help people and provide some with motivation to get better, it largely leaves people feeling invalidated and increases the urge to relapse. The recovery community on social media can be so great, but it is important to not become consumed by this content because it drives competition and leaves sufferers feeling triggered. One thing in particular that is especially damaging is 'What I eat in a day' videos. While these may be enjoyed by a lot of people with and without eating disorders, it is also essential that we all take these videos with a pinch of salt and try our best not to compare our diet to theirs. Just because someone you admire is eating a certain way, it does not mean you need to or should. In fact, mimicking other people's diets is neglecting your own needs. Remember, what other people eat, look like or do has nothing to do with you or what you need/should be doing. And if you feel like social media is actually doing more harm than good, take a break.

Keeping yourself motivated

As previously mentioned, commitment is your best friend in recovery, especially because of how fleeting motivation is. One of the hardest things about recovery is keeping yourself motivated. But how can you do that?

1. Look at photos of your younger self
2. Remind yourself of your reasons to recover (go back to when you wrote your reasons why in this journal)
3. Talk to someone close to you (ask them for reassurance that recovery is the right choice)
4. Challenge yourself! The best way to get out of a rut is to challenge yourself. Go back to when you listed your fear food challenge list and choose something off there!
5. Watch recovery YouTubers or listen to recovery podcasts ('The Recovery Club' of course)
6. Bake or cook following a recipe. Try something new and have a fun experience following a recipe. You can even ask someone to join you! Food can be an amazing opportunity to create memories.
7. Cry it out. If you are struggling and feeling overwhelmed, crying can be very helpful and is a healthy habit. Recovery is hard and you will have these days, so let them pass and know that better days are around the corner.

The initial weight gain

When you enter recovery, you may see that you have gained some weight. You may be panicking and you might start thinking that recovery was a bad decision. But here's the thing. The first time you face a fear will always be terrifying, and it won't be comfortable for you. But that doesn't mean that recovery will always feel this hard. Gaining weight gets less scary because you are repeatedly exposing yourself to your fear, and that means you are regaining your power. I know how terrifying that first initial weight gain is, so here is some guidance to help you manage what you may be experiencing:
"I need to lose the weight I have gained"
No you don't. I know that gaining weight has made you feel overwhelmed, stressed and perhaps regretful regarding choosing recovery, but this weight wasn't a mistake to gain. The weight you are gaining is a good thing, even though it feels wrong because your physical health improving makes it easier for you to focus on mentally healing, which is where recovery actually happens.

"I look so big, will everyone notice?"
It is definitely impossible for any weight you have initially gained to have changed the way you look so soon. We often believe that people notice when we gain weight, but it is actually not common for people to notice any physical changes unless it is an extreme change, but any initial weight gain would not be noticed.
"I look so much worse"

Our eating disorders influence what we perceive to be beautiful. When you were younger, you probably didn't think the most beautiful version of yourself was when you were sick, but maybe now you do. Maybe you think the most attractive thing you or anyone else could look like is sick, emaciated, thin, skinny, etc, and that you are your most beautiful self when you are sick, but that doesn't align with reality. Try something new by appreciating what you look like, and if that still doesn't help, then try something easier and focus on how your body functions for you. Focus on all the wonderful ways your body works for you, and try to zoom out on the way it looks. It's not always as easy as that, but challenge yourself by shifting your focus from looks to function.

The initial weight gain is always the hardest but remember, your body needs to change in order for you to restore your health and happiness. Gaining weight, and going up in clothing sizes, these are all important aspects of recovery and they do get much easier to handle. One day, you will even feel happy that you gained weight!

Eating more than others

In recovery, you are bound to eat more than others. In fact, it is encouraged. If you have ever restricted your intake as a result of your eating disorder then it is necessary that you are eating lots of food in recovery, and this may mean that you are eating more than others at times. Maybe you are eating dinner as a family and you have more on your plate (or you want to get more food) than everyone else. You may experience feelings of embarrassment and guilt and maybe you are dealing with the feeling that you are an imposter (refer back to earlier pages about imposter syndrome). Know that what you are feeling is very common among sufferers, and that you haven't done anything bad by eating more. If this is you, then try and remind yourself of your needs. You are suffering from an eating disorder and trying to get better, and this food is helping you repair your health and get your life back. Maybe you're worried about the calories you have consumed. If this is you then remind yourself that you need as many calories as you can get and that the more calories you consume, the better. You have gone through periods of restriction so it isn't unexpected for your body to be asking for large amounts of food. The best you can do is honour these cravings, especially when it means you are eating more than others because this will ultimately be the thing that challenges you and pushes you further in the right direction.

Was it a binge or did you just honour your hunger?

Bingeing in recovery from a restrictive eating disorder occurs when you have neglected your needs, these being emotional, nutritional, mental, etc. It is very common to experience periods of time when your appetite is increased and you may find yourself eating a lot of food in a short period of time. You may be questioning whether you just binged or not, so I will highlight the difference for you! Binge eating disorder is characterised by people eating large amounts of food without feeling like they are in control of what they are doing. This may include eating past fullness, knowing you need to stop but not feeling in control or like you have the power to stop. If you have eaten what you would deem a large amount of food, then how does this differ from a binge? Well, if you are in recovery from an eating disorder (that isn't binge eating disorder/bulimia) and you experience what you consider a binge, then ask yourself these questions:

1. Did you eat a large amount of food and felt out of control while doing it?
2. Did you feel like you could stop eating when you wanted to?
3. Did you eat this amount because of mental or physical hunger or was it induced by emotions?

These are some of the ways that help decipher whether it was a binge episode or not. Now, there are two possible answers. You did binge or you didn't, and neither is shameful or superior, so let's talk a bit more about what you might be feeling and how you can deal with both of these scenarios.

You didn't binge. Maybe you felt extremely mentally or physically hungry and decided to eat until you were satisfied. However, maybe the guilt has crept in and now your eating disorder thoughts are telling you that you just binged and that you should feel shameful. If this is you, then don't panic because you have already answered the question. You didn't binge. What you did do however was perhaps eat an amount of food that your eating disorder deems too much. The amount you ate was what felt right to you and was an act of satisfying your mental/physical hunger. What you did was a good thing, even though you may be feeling guilt and shame, so keep reminding yourself that what you did was a good thing. You may be panicking about gaining weight from what you ate. Well, it's helpful to know that the chance of you gaining weight from a single day is incredibly unlikely. But remember, even if you do gain weight, that is ultimately the goal. So if you are panicking about potentially gaining weight, then remind yourself that this is okay, and that you accept whatever bodily changes are necessary to your healing.

So, can you eat anything else or have you just eaten *too much?* No, you haven't eaten too much. If you are physically or mentally hungry, go and grab some food, and don't think about compensating the next day. Whatever you ate today doesn't dictate or influence what you eat tomorrow. You don't need to make up for eating more than usual, and you most definitely do not need to act upon urges to restrict, exercise or purge. If you are feeling overwhelmed and full, then try to sit with the discomfort. You don't need to do anything or act upon any urges, and you do not need to obsess over what you just ate. Try to sit with the uncomfortable feelings and let them pass, and remind you that they will pass. Everyone on this planet experiences feelings of fullness, you have nothing to feel guilty about and what you are experiencing is normal. I bet you felt fullness every day as a child growing up but you may not remember and that is because it was never challenging like it is now.

Envision your younger self eating. What did you use to enjoy eating? How did it make you feel? Did you feel happy? Did you eat to a point of fullness and not dwell on it? You wouldn't judge your younger self for eating their favourite foods and not caring about calories or weight. In fact, you may look back and envy your old relationship with food, where food was exciting and had no room for fear. Remind yourself that you are still that child, and that you can achieve a healthy relationship with food again and give that child what they deserve. Your inner child is still inside of you and you have the choice to serve it or neglect it. Food is an amazing way to reconnect to your true self and honour your inner child, and it is nothing to feel shame about. You are allowed to eat freely and without restriction, and through this, you are ultimately taking care of your inner child. It's always helpful to think of your younger self, so go and find some old photos or videos of you as a child and indulge in the idea that you are fully capable of having a healthy relationship with food again, just like you did when you were a child.

<u>You did binge</u>

Bingeing is a very overwhelming experience, and whether this is your first binge or you are familiar with them, it's important that you treat yourself kindly. It is very common to experience feelings of disgust and shame after or during a binge, but there is absolutely nothing to feel ashamed about. You just experienced an episode brought on by a mental disorder, none of this was your fault or something that you should feel guilty about. Binges are loosely defined as a loss of control, and it can be incredibly overwhelming to feel like you are not in the driver's seat of your own mind and body. But it is entirely possible to recover from binge eating disorder, as well as overcome the actual habit of bingeing itself. Bingeing is a very difficult thing to experience and it can leave you feeling incredibly tired and upset. To try and make the experience less overwhelming, here are some things that can help you recover from a binge!

1. Be kind to yourself

In all honesty, this is the most important piece of advice. The binge has happened, and you won't be feeling great as it is, so don't make it harder on yourself by dwelling or self-deprecating. It is in the past, you can't undo it, so the best thing you can do is accept that it happened, and acknowledge that you are going to keep trying to get better. All you can do is try your best, and sometimes things get the better of us. We won't always be perfect because there is no such thing. But if you can hold your head up high, accept that it has happened and try your best to take good care of yourself.

2. Hydrate

While it is very important that you take care of your mental health after a binge, it is also important that you take care of yourself from a physiological point of view. If some of the foods consumed during the binge were high in salt, then it is vital you hydrate to repair any electrolyte imbalances and aid in digestion.

3. Don't restrict

Often, binges are caused by periods of restriction. There is usually a cycle consisting of bingeing and restricting where a sufferer may restrict during the day only to binge at night, or perhaps you may binge and then restrict the next day. Having a restrictive diet is very harmful, and depriving yourself or certain foods or calories triggers overeating and intense cravings which may result in a binge episode.

4. Surround yourself with people

When you've binged, you might feel the urge to act upon behaviours. If you are feeling the urge to purge or exercise or hurt yourself in any way, find someone to sit with and don't let them out of your sight. If you are feeling the urge to hurt yourself, having someone around you will prevent anything bad from happening. So, get yourself out of the house, spend time with a family member or a friend, and keep yourself busy so it is easier to resist the urges.

Purging

If you've ever struggled with purging then you know too well just how addictive and debilitating this behaviour is. Purging is the act of making yourself vomit or exercising excessively. These episodes are often brought on by binges, but are not limited to this.

Post-binge purging is not triggered by the physical act of bingeing itself, but instead the emotions a binge provokes, such as guilt and shame. After a binge, you may experience strong negative feelings about yourself and the binge, and feel compelled to seek control in the form of purging (it is important to note that it is actually your eating disorder in control, and not you). Maybe you purge because you are feeling a lot of physical discomfort and want relief from it. Everyone has different reasons for acting on behaviours, but these are some of the common reasons one may purge following a binge. If you are someone who feels trapped in a restrict-binge-purge cycle, then you know just how difficult it is to break out. After a while, this cycle can become your new normal and you forget what it is like to have a healthy relationship with food. You may start planning binges and eating with the mental commitment of purging after. Maybe you feel like this will never end, that you will always be stuck in this cycle, but know that there is a way out of this cycle and it starts now.

There is no magic cure to help you stop purging. Everyone will have different motives for pursuing this behaviour so everyone will recover in their own

165

individual way. But one of the most helpful things you can do is break the restrict-binge-purge cycle. When you wake up in the morning, make a commitment to not restrict throughout the day. Make yourself a filling meal full of carbs, fats and proteins, and honour your hunger signals and cravings. If you are craving a fear food, maybe one that triggers a binge, remind yourself that you are not going down that road today, and that you can enjoy these foods without it leading to a binge and purge. No food is off-limits to you, and there are no good or bad foods. In the past, you may have eaten certain foods and then had a binge and purge episode, so now you subconsciously associate that food with bingeing. Because of this, you may try and avoid this food at all costs in fear of it causing a binge. While avoidance of trigger foods can prevent a binge in the short term, it will only lead to more binges in the future. You have committed to breaking the cycle, so now you must unlearn any associations you have made. It will help if you are able to see all food as neutral, instead of good and bad, to avoid restriction and ultimately break the restrict-binge-purge cycle.

If you want to overcome the restrict-binge-purge cycle, you have to stop viewing certain foods as off-limits and something to avoid. Instead, try and spend the day not restricting and honouring your cravings and hunger signals, and incorporate trigger foods. If you have a craving for a certain trigger food, allow yourself to eat it and remind yourself that you are not doing anything wrong and that you are allowed to eat as much as you want until you're satisfied. Try to ensure that your emotions don't run high and that you don't get overwhelmed, because feeling negative emotions towards and around food can very easily trigger a binge-purge episode.

If you've managed to not restrict today but still ended up bingeing, purging or both, then try not to panic. You might be losing hope and experiencing thoughts that tell you you're never going to get better, and that you will always be stuck in this cycle. This catastrophic thinking will hinder your progress, so try to avoid extremities and black-and-white thinking. This episode does not mean you've lost all of your progress, and you haven't failed. If you tell yourself that you have failed, you are setting yourself up and potentially hindering your recovery. Try your best to use positive affirmations to counterbalance the negative beliefs.

If you're lacking the motivation to overcome this behaviour, reminding yourself of some of the health consequences may help you understand the destructive nature of purging. Purging damages your physical and mental health in so many ways. It causes dehydration, facial swelling, irregular heartbeat, electrolyte imbalances and can be fatal. Let's break down some of the health consequences of purging.

Oral and digestive health

Purging takes a huge toll on your oral health. When you vomit, you are ultimately bringing up stomach acid which not only damages your teeth but can also contribute towards developing tooth sensitivity and gum disease. You may notice that your cheeks and jaw appear swollen, this is a side effect of purging but does go away with time when the behaviour is broken. The stomach acid you are bringing up has the potential to tear your oesophagus, irritate your stomach, and damage your intestines resulting in diarrhoea, constipation and bloating.

Heart and Circulatory system

Frequently purging causes extreme fatigue, weak muscles, dehydration and electrolyte imbalances which are incredibly threatening to the health of your heart. You may also experience an irregular heartbeat. But why? Purging removes many important electrolytes such as sodium, magnesium and potassium from the body, and the depletion of these electrolytes threatens your heart and kidney function. It might be a good idea to take electrolyte supplements while recovering from a purge to help your body restore lost necessities.

Reproductive system

Not only does purging cause electrolyte imbalances, but also hormonal imbalances. Purging can cause menstrual cycles to stop or become disrupted, and there is a higher chance of complicated pregnancies. The risk of premature births, caesarean deliveries and miscarriages massively increases and you may develop gestational diabetes.

Other physical effects include:

- low blood pressure
- trouble regulating body temperature
- acid reflux
- ingestion
- heartburn
- hoarse voice
- russell's sign
- hair, skin and nail problems
- pancreatitis

Mental effects include:

- irritability
- suicidal thoughts
- suicidal actions
- drug or alcohol dependency
- depression
- anxiety

Exercise

Science has proven the many benefits of exercise, and it is suggested that exercise is key to a balanced and healthy life. But what does this mean for people with eating disorders? Because obsessive exercise can be a symptom of an eating disorder, it is highly encouraged for sufferers of eating disorders to not partake in exercise. In fact, exercise poses many threats to our bodies and our minds.

Many of us may turn to exercise as a way to burn calories, feel in control, compensate, and punish ourselves. Everyone who struggles with an ED will have a different type of relationship with exercise, and it is important to know that not everyone with an ED exercises. If you are invalidating your ED because you do not exercise, please remember that everyone will have different experiences of the illness, and not everyone shares the same symptoms. The sickness of another is not the absence of your own sickness. If you struggle with an exercise obsession, you may experience feeling urges to exercise as an attempt to relieve mental stress. If you are not in a situation where you can exercise, you might feel overwhelmed and stressed and begin to panic. Perhaps you feel guilty for missing a workout or not reaching a goal you had set. If this resonates with you, it is likely that your relationship with exercise is very unhealthy. But why does it matter? Having an unhealthy relationship with exercise puts your body and mind under a lot of pressure. As eating disorders influence so many of our desires, goals and behaviours, it is difficult to determine whether your interest in fitness is genuine. Yes, fitness is supposed to benefit mental health, but that won't apply to those suffering with an ED. In fact, it would be more damaging to your mental health if you were to partake in fitness, than if you wouldn't. However, sometimes we don't think something is a problem (in this case, exercising and having an eating disorder) to our mental health because it might make us feel good, and thus make us believe it is benefiting our mental health. Our brains are complex, and it is important to know that good feelings do not always correlate to good choices or behaviours. In fact, eating disorders are very similar to addictions in the sense that engaging in them can bring about feelings of happiness. But this happiness may just stem from the act of feeding the addiction. So if engaging in exercise makes you feel good, then why would you want to stop?

Just because exercise makes you feel good, it doesn't mean it is good for you. Just because it is socially acceptable and massively encouraged in society, it doesn't mean that this behaviour is any less disordered than any other ED behaviour. If you want to recover, you will have to take a break from exercising to give your body the rest it needs to repair and recover, and to challenge the eating disorder. It doesn't mean that you will never be able to exercise again, it just means that for now your body and mind is in the middle of recovering from a very debilitating illness and exercise wouldn't benefit you right now. Take a break from exercise until you are in a much better place mentally and physically. But how do you stop?

1. Seek help

If you can, seek professional help. However, help isn't always accessible to everyone. There are many resources online that anyone can access for free, including podcasts (e.g. The Recovery Club), the recovery community, BEAT charity, NEDA, and many more. I will include a list of resources at the end.

2. Write down what your relationship with exercise is like

_____

_____

_____

_____

_____

_____

_____

_____

3. Write down your reasons for overcoming this behaviour

_____

_____

_____

_____

_____

_____

_____

_____

4. Discover the root of the behaviour

What is the purpose of this behaviour? What do you feel when you don't or can't exercise when you want to? What does exercising mean to you? What feelings does it distract you from? Every behaviour has a purpose, a cause, and getting to the bottom of what this is will give you the power to finally overcome this behaviour.

Use this space to journal your thoughts

_____

_____

_____

_____

_____

_____

_____

_____

_____

_____

_____

_____

_____

_____

_____

_____

5. Challenge your beliefs

Do you think that you will gain weight if you miss a workout? Are you scared that you will lose control if you stop exercising? Whatever your ED tells you that encourages you to engage in this disordered behaviour. try and challenge it.

"If I don't exercise then....

_____

_____

_____

_____

_____

_____

_____

Now try and rephrase this. Here's an example:

If I don't exercise, then I am allowing my body to heal and my mind to recover. Not exercising is an act of kindness to myself.

_____

_____

_____

_____

_____

_____

_____

_____

Diet Culture

The diet and fitness industry is a multi-billion-dollar industry that profits from people's desire to change the way they look. Of course, not everyone will have a disordered relationship with food, exercise or their bodies, but there is a large percentage of people who do. We live in a diet-obsessed society where calories and weight loss tips are everywhere, even on the sides of buses and TV adverts. It is almost impossible to avoid it, which makes recovering from an eating disorder so much more difficult. In fact, I assume that one of the many reasons so many people have disordered relationships with food is because of how embedded diet culture is in our minds. From the minute we are born we are being fed diet culture on a spoon, so it is no wonder that so many of us began engaging in ED behaviours before even developing an ED. Calorie counting and weight loss diets have become so normalised despite the dangers, and more and more children are becoming hyperaware of their diets and their bodies. Eating disorders are being encouraged through the normalisation of disordered eating and the glamourisation of thin bodies.

Diet culture is not concerned with your mental and physical health but instead focuses on promoting ways to change your body. Under the guise of health concerns, diet culture has been telling us how to change our bodies for decades. This culture tells us to cut out food groups, over exercise, restrict our intake, fast, eat lots of protein, eat low carb and low fat, etc. It promotes dangerous weight loss products and new ways to hate ourselves. Diet culture is toxic, there is no denying that. So how do we disassociate ourselves from it?

1.   Leave the conversation if it turns to diet talk

You can't always prevent people from talking about dieting, so step back and leave the conversation if that happens. Overhearing diet talk is very common, because like I said we live in a diet-obsessed society, so removing yourself from that environment will reduce the impact that conversation had on your mental health.

2.   Set boundaries

You are recovering from an eating disorder and have experienced the debilitating effects of diet culture. You have every right to ask that the people around you don't talk about dieting or weight loss in your presence. I know it can be difficult to set boundaries, but just asking them to not mention triggering things to you is important and necessary to protect your mental health. If you don't want to be so upfront, you could express how diet culture makes you uncomfortable, and hopefully, that will alert the other person to not engage in diet talk with you.

3.   You have different needs to what diet culture can offer you

Diet culture will exist forevermore, and as awful as that is, there are ways to reframe your thoughts when it begins to trigger you. Whenever you feel yourself becoming triggered by diet culture or diet-related talk, remind yourself that you have different needs to what diet culture can offer you. Your focus is recovery, and weight loss and dieting have absolutely no purpose for you. You don't need to learn how to *get lean* or *lose weight in 30 days* like diet culture often encourages. Instead, your focus is restoring your weight and recovering from a mental illness. You have no reason to listen to diet culture. Keep reminding yourself of this and this shall hopefully reduce the likelihood of you being triggered by diet culture.

4. Unfollow pages that promote diet culture

Social media has made it very difficult to avoid diet culture, as there are thousands of pages dedicated to promoting disordered eating. If you follow any accounts that either directly promotes dieting or weight loss, or even indirectly through an emphasis on body shape and weight, then please do yourself a favour and unfollow. On Instagram, you can filter our weight loss ads: go to settings, choose "ads", select "ad topics", you should see "body weight control" on there, and choose "see less". This should reduce the amount of weight-related or diet-related content!

5. Follow body-positive, and food-positive pages

Although there is a large amount of diet-focused content on social media, there are some amazing creators that promote body positivity and food freedom. What content you see influences your mood and way of thinking, so having more body-positive and food-positive content will be beneficial to your mood!

1. Write down your earliest memory of you being influenced by diet culture

_____

_____

_____

_____

_____

_____

_____

_____

_____

_____

2. Write down your experience of diet culture and how it has harmed you

_____

_____

_____

_____

_____

_____

_____

_____

_____

_____

3. How has diet culture impacted your daily life? *Think about how it influences your choices (e.g. food, activity, etc)*

4. Do you ever feel guilty about what you eat? How does diet culture account for this?

_____

_____

_____

_____

_____

_____

_____

_____

_____

_____

_____

_____

_____

_____

_____

_____

_____

_____

_____

_____

_____

_____

_____

There are no bad foods

A lot of us in recovery feel pressure to eat "healthily", high protein and "clean". While many of us give up calorie counting and restricting, we may develop an interest in "healthy" eating to compensate. This development may also be caused by our desire to be strong and lean as a way to deal with weight gain. The issue is, while you may think it is a positive thing to switch from restricting to ensuring that your meals are highly nutritious, it can be quite damaging. Switching from an obsession with restriction and weight loss, to an obsession with health and achieving a toned body is not an act of recovery, because you are substituting one disordered behaviour for another.

In recent years, protein has been placed on a pedestal and we are constantly being encouraged to eat large amounts of it. The issue with this is that it completely disregards the importance of other macronutrients such as carbohydrates and fats. All macros are essential and important and should be eaten in proper portions, so the glorification of protein is really just diet culture's latest attempt to demonise foods such as carbs and fats. No, you do not need to be eating excessive amounts of protein in a day, despite what social media encourages.

A lot of the time, people in recovery feel more confident eating healthified versions of "treats", such as protein bars instead of chocolate bars. You may find it easier to eat healthier versions of your favourite foods, but this doesn't necessarily mean it will be beneficial to your recovery. Avoiding your favourite foods is delaying food freedom, and is an act of self-punishment. Nothing bad will happen to you if you allow yourself what you want, and there is nothing wrong with these foods.

1. Have you ever avoided foods you love? If so, explain why.

_____

_____

_____

_____

_____

_____

_____

_____

_____

_____

_____

_____

_____

_____

_____

_____

_____

_____

2. What do you think about eating the foods you love? Do you feel guilty? Do you feel bad?

_____

_____

_____

_____

_____

_____

_____

_____

_____

_____

3. Write down why it is important for you to eat what you love

_____

_____

_____

_____

_____

_____

_____

_____

_____

_____

Now, put this to practise. Think of a food you love but have been avoiding. Now I want you to challenge your eating disorder and allow yourself to eat and enjoy this food.

How are you challenging yourself today?

Why are you challenging yourself?

What will you do differently?

How will you cope if it gets hard?

How did the challenge go?

_____

_____

_____

_____

_____

_____

_____

What did you observe yourself feeling?

_____

_____

_____

_____

_____

_____

_____

How did you cope?

_____

_____

_____

_____

_____

_____

How did you feel afterwards?

_____

_____

_____

_____

_____

_____

Food is medicine

You have probably heard the phrase 'food is medicine', and had someone tell you that a car can't drive without fuel, just like we can't function without food. These are very common recovery phrases but what do they mean? How can food cure a mental illness?

It can't. Eating food alone is not enough for you to recover from an eating disorder. What you need to do is heal your relationship with food, which can only be done through exposure, so food will be a key component of recovery. Food is your medicine in the sense that it provides nutrients and energy to you and aids your physical recovery. This physical recovery is responsible for mental recovery, because only when you're providing your body and brain with sufficient energy, can you mentally and cognitively function better. Ultimately, nourishing your body with sufficient energy will allow you to mentally and physically recover and improve the general state of your well-being. So, try to approach food from this perspective. See it as the medicine that allows you to improve your relationships, both with yourself and food.

If food is medicine, then why do some of us struggle with our mental health despite physical signs of recovery (e.g. weight gain, regulated hunger cues, non-restrictive diet, etc)? You can feel cheated when you have gained weight and have not noticed any mental changes. It may make you regret recovering because you are still mentally in the same place as you were before recovery.

Don't panic, this is very normal and commonly experienced. I believe physical recovery usually happens before mental recovery. Usually, it usually takes less time to weight restore than it does to mentally recover, but as I've previously stated, everyone differs. If this is the case and you're wondering if you will ever feel better mentally, find reassurance in the fact that things can get better. Recovering from an eating disorder doesn't prevent other traumatic or tragic things from happening in your life, but the eating disorder won't be one of those things anymore and so, yes, things will get better if you continue to recover.

Gaining weight but not feeling better?

This is an extremely common experience for sufferers of eating disorders. The benefits of weight gain on mental health are constantly being preached, but what if you don't feel any better? What if you feel just as bad or even worse than you did before recovery? It's common to experience feeling cheated, regretful about gaining weight, and scared by your fading hope. But please remember that recovery is a process and it takes time. There will be times when you are feeling mentally better and possess a more positive mindset about recovery, and then there will be times when you may regret recovery and resent yourself for gaining weight. Recovery is hard, and there will be challenges where you may even be tempted to turn back and relapse, but mental recovery is possible. Give yourself time, don't give up on recovery because you're losing hope. Keep going because there is freedom on the other side of recovery.

A reason why you may feel mentally worse while having weight restored is that eating disorders are often caused by trauma, unresolved difficult emotions and negative belief systems. If you haven't worked through the emotions that caused you to rely on your eating disorder to cope, then you're preventing mental healing and you're more likely to be trapped in a recovery-relapse cycle. See the previous chapter, 'Relapse vs Recovery'.

Focus your attention on improving your mental health by addressing any underlying negative beliefs about yourself, and any trauma you have experienced and finding your reasons for depending on an eating disorder to cope. Yes, engaging in eating disorders can become normal and habitual, but there will be things that you need to address from your past, and things that may even seem unconnected to your eating disorder but still hold power over you.

1. Is there anything that you believe could have influenced the development of your eating disorder?

_____

_____

_____

_____

_____

_____

_____

_____

_____

_____

_____

_____

_____

_____

_____

_____

2. What beliefs, thoughts, feelings and experiences need addressing to help you move forward in your recovery?

_____

_____

_____

_____

_____

_____

_____

_____

_____

_____

_____

_____

_____

_____

_____

This is not easy and requires a lot of vulnerability and dedication. You are on an emotional scavenger hunt and it is going to be thought-provoking and may even bring about overwhelming emotions. It may be painful diving deeper into who you are and what you have been through, so be gentle and take it slow. Don't overwhelm yourself with more than you feel you can handle. Healing is painful and can often feel catastrophic. Keep yourself safe and treat yourself kindly. What you are doing is amazing and incredibly brave. Give yourself credit!

Dealing with comments on your weight

Weight gain is both a necessary and difficult part of recovering from a restrictive eating disorder, and sometimes people may make comments about it. You might have been told how much healthier you look, and while this sounds innocent, it can leave you feeling invalid and increase urges to relapse. Being told you look better is not the compliment people may think it is, especially because EDs create a desire to look and be sick. So, how do you prevent being triggered when someone makes unwanted comments about your weight?

In a perfect world, weight wouldn't be a topic people tend to talk about, but we live in a very superficial society where weight is obsessed over. If someone makes a comment about your weight or the weight you have gained, here are some ways to respond:

1. Recognise the intention of this comment

If this comment was said by someone close to you, try to understand that this person has probably spent a lot of time worrying over you, and they may perceive your weight gain to mean you are getting better, which to them is an amazing thing. However, weight gain doesn't always equate to improved mental health, so while this comment was intended to be positive, you may perceive it to be negative. Remind yourself that the intention was good, and that their comment has no hidden underlying meaning. This comment isn't meant as a judgement, but as a compliment.

2. "You look healthy" ≠ "You look big"

For many of us, hearing "you look healthy" automatically translates to "you look big". But why is this? If weight loss was a side effect of your eating disorder, you may have initially received positive comments and praise for it. This positive reinforcement teaches us that we will receive praise and attention if we lose weight, and so this fuels our desire to lose more weight. In recovery, you are gaining weight instead. If you have learned that losing weight is a good thing through reinforcement, then you will associate gaining weight with failing. When someone says "you look healthy", we associate these words with gaining weight and perceive it to be a negative thing, void of praise and attention.

3. Ways to respond

If you don't know how to exactly respond to the comment, then here are some good examples:

*"Oh thank you" *Change the subject**
"Please don't comment on my weight, it makes me uncomfortable"
"Would you mind if we changed the subject?"
"I understand you meant well but that is hard for me to hear"
"Weight isn't an indicator of how well someone is doing"

4. Don't feel bad for setting boundaries

You are allowed to ask people to not make comments on your appearance without feeling guilty for doing so. This is your recovery and it is important to protect it. Those who care will take this on board and hopefully will do better in the future to prevent triggering you.

It's not easy hearing people discuss your appearance when you are so judgemental and hyperaware of your body as it is. Gaining weight and having your appearance change is going to be a challenge because it is new for you, and it will take some time to adjust so be patient with yourself. You've got this.

1. How does it make you feel when people comment on your body?

_____

_____

_____

_____

_____

_____

_____

_____

_____

_____

_____

_____

_____

_____

2. Does being told you look healthy affect you? How?

_____

_____

_____

_____

_____

_____

_____

_____

One thing about perceiving "you look healthy" negatively and associating it with judgments about weight gain, is that it only really applies to you. If you see someone who you perceive to be looking healthier, would you be judging them or would you be happy that they were recovering? Most likely the latter. So why is it any different when it comes to you? If you look at other people in recovery and feel happy that they are getting better and weight restoring, then why is looking healthy a bad thing? Looking healthier is not a bad thing at all, it is a good thing, only the eating disorder doesn't want you to get better and plants beliefs in your brain that are not backed up by logic and reason. EDs lose power over us if we believe that looking healthier is a great thing, so challenge yourself by asking whether the intention of these comments is positive, or if the ED is just trying to control you through demonising recovery and weight gain. It's the latter.

Use this space to journal your thoughts:

Do you have internalised fatphobia?

Internalised fatphobia refers to internalised oppression and hatred for larger bodies and weight gain. Maybe you've looked in the mirror and felt like you were less unattractive because you gained weight or looked bloated, or maybe just perceived your body in a distorted way and didn't like it (most likely the case if you suffer from body dysmorphia). These are all examples of internalised fatphobia. But where does fatphobia come from?

There has been a social stigma of obesity for too long, particularly in the Western world, where society prefers bodies that represent health and fertility. People with larger bodies typically tend to experience discrimination and prejudicial assumptions in all societal settings. From discriminative medical treatment to everyday glares from strangers in restaurants, people with larger bodies have had it all. And while we have become progressive as a society, fatphobia is still very prevalent in our society. From weight-loss ads to introducing the calories in the menus in England, fatphobia is everywhere, so it's no wonder we have internalised this. Through society's torment of people in larger bodies, we have learned that to be big is a shameful thing. This learned shame is a seed that plants insecurity and a desire to lose weight (or maintain a low-to-normal weight) in our heads. We grow up becoming increasingly aware of calories and clothing sizes, and it is only being fuelled by the everyday fatphobia that we encounter. But if everyone has internalised fatphobia, then what's the big deal about you having it?

Internalised fatphobia contributes towards the development of most eating disorders, and it is often what prevents us from recovering. The fear of weight gain is caused by many factors, but the internalisation of fatphobia makes many of us afraid of how other people will react to our weight gain and validates our beliefs that skinny is superior. It's key that you challenge your internalised fatphobia to overcome the beliefs and fears that hinder your recovery. If you can tackle the root of why you are so scared to gain weight, then maybe you can overcome the fear and start living your life.

1. What was your earliest memory of being aware that larger bodies are at a disadvantage in our society?

2. Did you ever experience someone close to you (maybe a parent, sibling, friend or relative) being judgmental towards their weight or perhaps being on a diet?

3. At What age did you begin to worry about your weight? What was that like?

_____

_____

_____

_____

_____

_____

_____

_____

_____

_____

_____

_____

_____

_____

_____

_____

_____

_____

_____

_____

_____

4. How does it make you feel thinking about your younger self and their relationship with their body?

_____
_____
_____
_____
_____
_____
_____
_____
_____
_____
_____
_____
_____
_____
_____
_____
_____
_____
_____
_____
_____

5. Why are you afraid to gain weight?

_____

_____

_____

_____

_____

_____

_____

_____

_____

_____

_____

_____

_____

_____

_____

_____

_____

_____

_____

_____

_____

_____

_____

Eating disorders as an aesthetic

Before you developed an eating disorder, you probably pictured someone who suffered from one as an emaciated white teenager. But where did this stereotype come from? Unsurprisingly, the media is responsible for the existence of this stereotype, as the very limited number of films and documentaries about eating disorders picture a thin, white teenage girl. But self-produced media is also responsible.

Many pro-eating disorder communities idolise the likes of Kate Moss and Lily-Rose Depp, with their image being used as thinspiration. EDs have become an aesthetic on social media which is incredibly dangerous, and platforms such as TikTok, Instagram, Twitter and Tumblr have many young users who are being exposed to a glamorised version of a deadly illness. It will also trigger those with an eating disorder, and this can be particularly dangerous for those in recovery.

'Heroin Chic' was a style that became popular in the 1990s, when drug abuse and eating disorders were very prevalent in model culture, and is characterised by emaciated bodies, dark circles and pale skin (all traits associated with drug abuse). This style came around as a sort of rebellion against the 1980s "clean girl" aesthetic, with popular models in the 80s such as Cindy Crawford and Claudia Schiffer defining beauty as vibrance and good health. Heroin chic took over the fashion industry and seeped its way into society, encouraging young girls to aspire to look sick and develop drug addictions. This style began to fade out when everyone's attention turned to the Kardashians, and curvy bodies came to be favoured over thin bodies. This is also in line with the return of the "clean girl" aesthetic, and judging by the pattern, it is no surprise that heroin chic is on its way back.

The return of heroin chic is terrifying for people in recovery. Gaining weight and weight restoration is difficult enough, but to have society praise the body type that you are trying to let go of can feel impossible. It is already difficult enough trying to accept your weight-restored body, but to have to go through this in a society that glorifies your smaller body makes it that much harder. However you are feeling about this latest comeback, remember that this doesn't mean you have to focus your attention on losing weight. Your smaller body is not your superior body, and you do not have to indulge in body trends. Your body is not a trend and it is incredibly insensitive for people to enable this horrific style to come back despite how progressive society has come in regard to mental health awareness. Eating disorders are deadly, and you have to protect your recovery by ignoring our ever-changing beauty standards. Trends come and go, but what is constant is your need to be healthy and commit to recovery.

Lack of diversity and representation

Before you had an eating disorder, you probably pictured someone with one looking like a white, straight, thin teenager. Why? Because the media has consistently portrayed ED sufferers like this. There is a huge lack of diverse representation and this can leave many sufferers feeling invalid and may even give some people imposter syndrome, and it's no surprise. If you develop an illness that is **presented** as affecting predominantly white, underweight teenagers, then it's no wonder you feel like a fraud if you don't mirror this stereotype. The truth is that eating disorders affect everyone, regardless of age, weight, gender, ethnicity, sexual orientation and race.

Those who are black, indigenous or people of colour (BIPOC) are shown to be treated at much lower rates than white people. In fact, doctors are less likely to ask BIPOC individuals about ED symptoms, with a 50% less chance of receiving a diagnosis or treatment. But why is this? Systematic racism, stereotypes and an underfunded healthcare system leave BIPOC individuals disadvantaged, and the lack of diverse representation only adds to this.

I wanted to speak to someone and have them share their own personal experience of living with an eating disorder and being a woman of colour.

"What has your experience been like living with an eating disorder as a BIPOC individual?"

I would say that I have definitely felt marginalised and like I was "other". Suffering with an eating disorder is already isolating enough without feeling like I am being treated differently than any other white patient would be. I probably would have started recovering sooner had my eating disorder been taken more seriously. The treatment I have received has made me feel like I am less deserving of help, and that I am not sick enough. I feel like I am at a constant disadvantage.

"What has your experience of treatment been like?"

I've been belittled a lot by professionals and it's clear to me that professionals treated me differently than any other white patient. There is a lot of medical gaslighting and invalidation involved, and it makes me feel like I am different, or that I have a different eating disorder from a white person because of the differences in treatment. Between long waiting lists and being invalidated when I reached out for much-needed support, it's easy to feel like a fraud.

"How would you say the media's portrayal of eating disorders has affected you?"

It's hard. I am constantly comparing myself to eurocentric beauty standards and as a person with an eating disorder, I am already comparing myself to everyone, so it just makes it even more difficult. The "perfect" anorexic is

206

portrayed as this extremely thin white teenager, and I can't mirror that, so it feels like I am automatically set up to not feel enough.

"Do you feel you have a good support system?"

It's a hard question to answer because black culture shies away from conversations about mental health, and while it is getting better, you're almost made to feel ungrateful for turning down food. Food is a big part of my culture and I definitely feel like I have lost touch with that because of my eating disorder. Eating disorders aren't understood as much, and so I almost felt embarrassed for suffering and asking for help.

"What advice would you give to BIPOC individuals who suffer from an eating disorder?"

If food is big in your family or community, then embrace it. Try to reconnect with your culture and find people similar to you, who don't make you feel different. Remind yourself that your differences are the best part of you, and you do not have to change a single thing about yourself to conform, especially not to eurocentric beauty standards. You are perfect just as you are.

Therapy only works if you work with it

The truth is, nobody can recover for you. I used to think that I could self-destruct as much as I wanted and it wouldn't matter because my treatment team could save me. They could force me to gain weight and I wouldn't have to do it myself. They would always be there for me... right? But then I learned an incredibly valuable lesson: you have to do it yourself. I had therapy a couple of hours a week, and I would base my entire week around these sessions, and more specifically, these weigh-ins. Because I was in treatment for anorexia, I believed I had to maintain the eating disorder and treat weigh-ins like I had to lose weight to deserve their help. But the thing is, I really didn't. My therapists were doing a great job, but I used to think they wanted me to lose weight, and that every appointment was a test of my diagnosis. So I treated every therapist I've ever had like they were the judges in my sick ED competition. I craved medical validation, and my eating disorder turned therapy into a game. How sick can I become? How much weight can I lose before admission? Therapy was a huge part of my life, but for all the wrong reasons. And why? Because I didn't utilise therapy the right way. I would go to every session as if it was school and I was the kid in the back of the class who would do no work and expect a good grade. If I wanted to get better, I had to put in the work. Therapy can only work when you are working with it, instead of against it. Your therapist's job is to provide support and ensure your safety and well-being, they're not there to judge you or challenge your ED. If they're a good therapist, they're going to want you to get better. They won't be judging you for gaining weight like your ED makes you believe, they will be rooting for you because your well-being is in their best interest. The thing is, you have to cooperate in therapy if you want outcomes. It takes a lot of hard work and requires vulnerability to sort through your difficulties, but you have the strength. Yes, change is hard. Recovery feels impossible some days. but, it's worth it.

Nobody can force you to recover. They can force you to gain weight but nobody can change your mindset for you. If you want to overcome the eating disorder, you're going to have to do it yourself. In some people's cases, you might be at a point where you're being threatened with more specialist care. If this is you, try your best to cooperate. Only you have the power to change things around, to achieve food freedom and recovery from your mental health issues.

Realising that you are fully responsible for your own recovery is a huge but necessary step in your recovery. People can't make you recover, you have to do it yourself.

The glorification of hospitalisation

Only a small percentage of patients with EDs get hospitalised, and yet the majority seem to view hospitalisation as an ED goal. The idea that hospitalisation is the ultimate goal stems from a desire to be as sick as possible. There will be underlying issues that create that desire and it will definitely need addressing in your recovery.

There is a huge focus on hospitalisation on social media, and it appears to be something that a lot of people desire. If you are suffering from an ED and haven't been hospitalised, it is likely that you experience feeling like you need to be hospitalised to be valid. But the thing is, hospitalisation is not some reward for being the best at an ED. It is a **form** of treatment, and it is not superior to any other form of treatment. In fact, hospitalisation is incredibly traumatic for some. There is no denying its effectiveness in stabilising patients, but it is an incredibly invasive and intense form of treatment that is not to be desired or glorified. There seems to be the notion that individuals who are hospitalised are sicker than those who are not, but this isn't true, and definitely not a helpful way of thinking. Try to stop seeing other people as your competition, it isn't you against them, and it definitely isn't a contest of "who's the best anorexic/bulimic/etc." Everybody's experience and treatment of their eating disorder will be individual to them. If you haven't been hospitalised, you are not inferior or less valid than someone who has. In fact, the vast majority of sufferers have never been hospitalised, and that doesn't mean the majority of us shouldn't recover. Don't let social media or your eating disorder glorify hospitalisation. Remind yourself of the reality of what life is like in a hospital, and use that to deter you away from striving for it.

1. Have you ever wanted to be hospitalised? Why?

_____

_____

_____

_____

_____

_____

_____

_____

_____

_____

_____

_____

_____

_____

_____

_____

_____

_____

Are you in control?

A lot of things in our lives are not within our control, and this can be difficult to process. In my experience, things felt very out of control for me when my dad was diagnosed with motor neurone disease, a terminal illness. This loss of control made me want it even more, and so I used food to regain feelings of control in my life. We are all under the notion that developing an eating disorder gives us some control over our lives, but are we really in control?

Eating disorders tell us what to do, controlling every aspect of our lives from what is on our plate (or not on our plate), to who we become as a friend, a child, a sibling, and as a person. We believe if we control our weight then we are restoring some sort of lost control, but we're actually **giving up** control this way. By surrendering to the demands of your eating disorder, you are a servant to it, dedicating your life to pleasing an illness that only wants you dead. If we were really in control like our EDs make us believe, then we would be able to stop caring. We would be able to turn our EDs off like a switch. Unfortunately, we can't, and this is because our eating disorders are controlling us, instead of the other way around.

We like to think that we are invincible, that we can self-destruct as much as we want but nothing bad will happen to us (e.g. death from an ED) because we "are in control". But we're not, and negative life-changing consequences could arise in anyone, regardless of age, weight, etc. It is like the eating disorder is driving the car, and we are in the passenger seat. We become observers of our own lives, watching as our eating disorders take over and drive us down dangerous roads while we sit back and watch everything crash and burn. But it is time to regain control, to jump back in the driving seat of your own life and change directions. You have explored the route of an eating disorder, and I can imagine it hasn't been a walk in the park. So now, why don't you try a different direction? Grab hold of the steering wheel and turn things around for the better. You are fully capable of being in control of your own life, but restricting food and self-destructing is not the method to do so.

1. Why do you feel out of control in your life?

_____

_____

_____

_____

_____

_____

_____

_____

_____

_____

_____

_____

_____

_____

_____

_____

_____

_____

_____

_____

_____

2. Are you really in control of your eating disorder, or is your eating
   disorder controlling you?

_____

_____

_____

_____

_____

_____

_____

_____

_____

_____

_____

_____

You have a life to be well for

It sounds silly, but you really do. In 40 years, you will look back and only have a handful of positive memories to dwell on if you never recover. Your best memory will be a time you allowed yourself a piece of cake, and to be honest, that doesn't sound very exhilarating.

When you're engaging in your eating disorder, your life becomes so small. You lose your spark and your personality is dominated by food. It feels like life has lost colour, and everything becomes so dull and bleak. Your relationships become strained, you find yourself isolating yourself to focus on your ED, and days just pass you by. When you're so focused on something, everything else becomes far less important and so your priorities will change. You don't have time for fun anymore, it requires too much energy and you can't remember the last time you belly laughed. Maybe you are content with this lifestyle, or maybe you are just scared of recovering.

But what about your younger self? What did you use to dream of becoming or doing with your life? What about all the places you want to travel to, or all the foods you want to eat? What job do you want? What is on your bucket list? I can imagine you haven't really asked yourself these questions as much since you developed an ED. Your future becomes less important when you're focusing on food. But it is important you ask yourself these questions to rediscover your passion for life.

215

1. What did your younger self dream of becoming?

_____

_____

_____

_____

_____

_____

_____

_____

_____

_____

_____

_____

_____

_____

_____

_____

_____

_____

_____

_____

_____

_____

_____

_____

2. Where did you younger self want to travel to?

3. What would your younger selves' bucket list look like?

4. Have you done as much as you've wanted to?

Asking yourself these questions will hopefully make you realise how much of your life is still left to be lived. You don't want to get older and have regrets about never recovering and never living your life to its fullest potential. It goes without saying that you will never regret recovery when you're 70 and looking back at your life. That is, of course, if you choose to recover.

You may convince yourself that you'll be fine, that you can still live a fulfilling life with an eating disorder, but is that really what you want? Do you really want to spend every day for the rest of your life consumed by food? I can imagine that would be a miserable existence. Look, you have a life to be well for. Your purpose is far more than self-destructing. You have countries to travel to, things to do, and even just the everyday mundane aspects of life can be so much more fulfilling. You deserve a life of abundance, you can be anything you want to be. If you want to spend the rest of your life committed to your eating disorder, go ahead. But you know deep down that is not the most fulfilling path you can take in life. Every time you feel urged to relapse or not begin recovery, remember this: You have a life to be well for, and it is waiting on the other side of recovery.

Missing your smaller body

Maybe you're feeling like you want to go back in time and never recover. It is normal to feel this way. In fact, one of the hardest parts of recovery is dealing with times when you miss your old body, or your eating disorder in general.

Usually, there is a much deeper understanding of why you miss your ED. Do things in your life feel out of control? Are you struggling with body image? Do you feel less valid now? Whatever the reason for missing your ED, that is the thing that needs addressing. No, you don't need to go back and undo all the hard work you've put into recovery. The issue isn't your body (it never has been). Use the "ask why" method I have previously discussed to discover the root of these feelings. Why do you miss your smaller body? Why do you miss your eating disorder?

If you're feeling out of control → remind yourself you were never in control to begin with when it comes to your eating disorder, and relapsing definitely won't give you any control.

If you're struggling with body image → Go back to the chapter on body image and reread or write down the journal entries related to the chapter.
If you're not feeling good enough → Your eating disorder never really made you feel any better. In fact, it probably made you feel worse. The euphoria that engaging in your ED gave you was always so fleeting, but recovery can give you long-term contentment and happiness.

If you're triggered → Ask yourself what triggered you, and why it did. Was it comparison? Do you feel invalid? Whatever it is, challenge your thoughts by changing your perspective.

The most helpful thing you can do for yourself at this moment is to remind yourself of the reality of the illness. It wasn't easy, it wasn't fun, and it was miserable and isolating. Do you want to feel miserable and isolated? If the answer is yes, then this is what you need to address. Why do you want to feel bad? Are you looking for sadness and pain because it is comforting? Are you seeking sadness because you believe you don't deserve to be happy?

1. Identify why you think you miss your eating disorder

_____

_____

_____

_____

_____

_____

_____

_____

_____

_____

Remember your reasons for beginning recovery. You wouldn't have started to recover if life engaging in your eating disorder was going well. You needed a change, you needed to recover and you still do. Going back won't change anything. Your experience won't be any better than the first time, and in the end, you will ultimately have to recover, so why go back? Why go back only to end up back where you are? Why don't you focus your energy on maintaining recovery and overcoming this obstacle? You are fully capable of doing it, you just have to keep pushing through. You can do this.

1. Use this space to journal your thoughts

Take it one meal at a time

Look, recovery is difficult. Some days you won't have the energy to give it your all, and that is okay. You need to take each hour at a time, each meal as it comes. Recovery doesn't have a fixed time limit, it isn't linear either, so don't be hard on yourself if you're struggling more than you expected (or the opposite, and you actually are doing better than you thought!). Take it at your own pace and remember, you are going to be okay.

Recovery is the best decision you will ever make. Maybe it doesn't feel so good, but it will. Just give it time, be patient and trust the process. Who knows how your life will turn out, but recovery opens all the doors back up for you, so really the unknown is exciting. But don't worry if you're overwhelmed. Like I said, take it one meal at a time.

You are fully capable of recovery, and you are fully deserving of it too. No matter what you weigh, your experience, or how others have treated you and your ED, you are **valid**, you are **sick enough** and you have a beautiful life ahead of you, filled with unlimited opportunities.

It is time to let your eating disorder go for good.

Your questions answered!

"When will I know what my set-point weight is?"

Your set-point weight takes a long time to establish, so don't overthink it too much. When you have weight restored, your body may fluctuate up and down, and you may find that your body naturally sets around a certain weight. The first step is weight restoration, involving you regaining the weight you lost due to your ED (if you lost weight). Only then can you find out your true set-point weight. However, IT WILL CHANGE! As we get older, our weight will fluctuate as normal. This is okay, and this is a normal part of growing up. But your body will settle into a set-point weight at some point, so keep going. If your body is still changing, if you're still gaining, then this is clear you're not at your set-point weight yet.

"Was weight gain as scary as you thought?"

Initially, yes. The first part of weight gain was terrifying to me, but over time it grew less important and definitely became less scary. My life started to expand because of recovery and truthfully, I finally wanted to be alive, so I didn't mind the weight gain. In the end, I feel grateful for the weight I have gained. It isn't always like this, it changes every day, but no matter how bad I feel or how difficult recovery is, I don't regret gaining weight. It gave me my life back. So to answer your question, no, weight gain is not as scary as I thought.

"How do you trust your body again?"

I love this question, even though it is a difficult one to provide one simple answer to. You have to trust the process. The human body is incredibly intelligent and works **for** us, not **against** us. So try to trust it. Trust that honouring your hunger cues won't lead to a binge. Trust that eating won't make you gain masses of weight overnight, but more importantly. trust that you are strong enough to deal with whatever comes your way. Your body will repair itself, but only if you are giving it what it needs. Your body isn't cruel for asking for lots of energy from you, it **needs** this energy to repair itself, so trust your body and give it the energy it needs.

"Will recovery make me happy?"

Well, nobody knows if it'll make you happy, but it will make your life easier, and the things that make you happy can be enjoyed. Happiness is on the other side of recovery. but if you're not feeling happy in your recovery, know that you're not done yet. Recovery will bring so much to your life, and it is definitely something worth pursuing.

"How long does it take for bloating to go away?"

Bloating is experienced by every single human on this planet. It serves a physiological function and is actually a good sign that your body is functioning correctly. Yes, it feels uncomfortable and yes, it may make your body image worse, but remember that everyone experiences bloating and that it is normal. I can't say bloating goes away permanently, but if you are referring to the extreme bloating that is commonly experienced in recovery, then it does get better.

When you're bloated, a common fear is that you'll never get rid of it and you will forever exist with a swollen tummy. But this isn't reality. Yes, you may wake up most days in recovery with a bloated stomach, but there is a reason. If your body has been through a period of starvation, your body will stop trusting you as much and will "cling on" to nutrients that you provide it, much like a caveman or an animal who goes long periods of time without energy resources. Your body attempts to insulate your most vital organs in an attempt to preserve your health and keep you alive. A lot of our most vital organs are in the midsection of our bodies, so of course, this is where you will experience the most bloating as your body attempts to store nutrients. If you're wondering if it will ever resolve itself, it will. Your body is smart. Give it time to heal and repair and soon enough the bloating will subside.

"When can I consider myself recovered?"

I suppose it differs for everyone, but I always imagined being recovered to present itself as talking about your eating disorder is past tense.
Some indicators of being recovered:

- The things that once used to govern your life are now so insignificant to you.
- You have an appreciation for your body and food
- You are not engaging in any disordered behaviours
- Things that used to challenge you are no longer challenging

Of course there are many more indicators of being recovered, but here are just a few!

From the author....

Writing this journal has been a huge challenge for me. It has forced me to confront a lot of areas of my own recovery that need working on, and I hope it has the same effect on you.

I wrote this journal because I believe everyone deserves help and equal access to it, but there isn't, and so I wanted to create something that anyone could get their hands on. This recovery journal is for everyone who has ever struggled with disordered eating and/or an eating disorder. I hope it challenges and comforts you and pushes you to ask yourself questions you haven't asked yet.

This journal was inspired by you. I have received so many lovely thoughtful messages regarding my podcast and I wanted to give you something that can assist your recovery.

I am so grateful for every single person who has supported me, strangers or friends, we are all in this together. Now I will pass this book on to you. I hope it challenges you beyond what you believed you could manage. You are stronger than you know.

Em xxx

List of resources

BEAT Eating Disorder Charity

website: www.beateatingdisorders.org.uk

helpline open 365 days (9am to 12am)

- England number: 0808 801 0677

- Scotland number: 0808 801 0432

- Wales number: 0808 801 0433

- Northern Ireland number: 0808 801 0434

email support

- England email: help@beateatingdisorders.org.uk

- Scotland email: scotlandhelp@beateatingdisorders.org.uk

- Wales email: waleshelp@beateatingdisorders.org.uk

- Northern Ireland email: NIhelp@beateatingdisorders.org.uk

National Eating Disorders Association

website: www.nationaleatingdisorders.org

About the author

Hi, I am Emily Donoher, the author of this book and the host of The Recovery Club podcast on apple podcasts and spotify. I am nineteen and I have suffered from different eating disorders for the last four years. I began recovery in April 2021 which is when I began sharing my recovery journey on social media. the recovery community embraced me and it is there where I have met many brave and inspiring people who are also in recovery from an eating disorder. I was very lucky to have received such amazing support from therapists, doctors, nurses and my family and close friends, yet I know how scarce resources are and how many people are left to their own devices without any support. The lack of resources was a huge problem for me, and so I decided to create my podcast, 'The Recovery Club', so everyone could have access to some support.

Over the last 6 months, I have poured my heart and soul into helping other people through my podcast, which is why I am so excited to finally give you this book.

My Journey

I have suffered with mental health issues since I was a young teenager, but it was around the age of fifteen that I developed disordered eating. I had a very obsessive and unhealthy relationship with my health which affected my eating and I began to become avoidant. I was struggling with an eating disorder but I didn't know it at the time because I was in denial that my obsession with health had become unhealthy.

I began counselling for my anxiety and disordered eating, and it was in CAMHs where I would later be diagnosed with anorexia nervosa. My struggles with food and obsession with health began to improve, but then things in my life started going wrong and I felt like I had no control over anything. My loving dad became terminally ill in 2019 to 2020 and it was then that my anorexia took full force. An eating disorder is a horrible thing to experience. It was very damaging to my family who were already going through so much, but it was my source of control. It allowed me to focus on something other than what was not in my control, and it gave me false feelings of peace.

I started with CAMHs (child and adolescent mental health services) for a couple years, which I personally didn't think benefited my recovery but I still am grateful for my care team there. There was so much going on in my life at that time. I became a young carer for my dad, who had just been diagnosed with Motor Neuron Disease (MND), and the country had just gone into lockdown. I was actually quite grateful for lockdown because it let me spend every second with my dad which looking back in retrospect, I am very grateful for. We knew dad was going to die soon, MND is an incurable terminal illness, but we didn't know when. Being a young carer was very difficult, physically and emotionally. I had to become a nurse for my dad, feeding and clothing him, helping him stand up, dealing with his catheter, hoisting him into bed, putting on his oxygen mask and watching him on a baby-monitor at night. It was a lot, but my Mum and Sister were amazing. We were a team, and while it was important to look after my dad physically, it was paramount that we made him feel good emotionally. If you don't know, MND is a disease that takes away your ability to walk, talk, move, and eventually breathe. It was a lot to process mentally, and I used my eating disorder to cope with it. Towards the end of his life, dad was in the hospital and none of us could see him due to the covid restrictions. I tried my best to get better at this point, but when he died in June 2021, I didn't care about recovering and this triggered a big relapse.

I was then transferred to the specialist adult eating disorder team, and again, I was very lucky with my team. I had a great relationship with them all which made therapy more effective for me. As well as struggling with an anorexia relapse, I was massively struggling with anxiety and depression, and in December 2021, I was admitted to my local psychiatric ward's home treatment team (HTT). This was on christmas day. I was due to be admitted but there was covid on the ward, so I did my best in the week that the ward was on lockdown, to turn things around. Thankfully, my doctor agreed to a treatment plan that meant I was allowed to stay at home. I had daily nurse

235

visits and couldn't go to college so my days were very empty and dull. There were two nurses who would frequently visit me and ended up becoming my head nurses, and it was these two who really changed my life. They got me to see that there was a point in recovery and in keeping myself safe, and it was some advice these nurses gave me that made me choose to commit to recovery. As horrible as this period of my life was, I remind myself that I wouldn't be where I am today, writing this book, if I didn't go through all of that.

Since January 2022, I have been committed to recovery. I was finally discharged from HTT and went back to school. I was getting better, I was actually recovering, which is something I never believed was possible for me. I was still under the care of the ED specialist team, but I no longer found it was helping me so I discharged myself in the Summer.

Recovery has been a very difficult journey, but I am so grateful for it. My life has colour again, and although things are not rainbows and sunshine, recovery has made my life so much brighter and more meaningful. I feel like a completely new person because of recovery, and this is why I am so passionate about helping others. I know that recovery is wonderful, and I want to share this with others and hopefully inspire them to commit themselves to recovery.

I am now in university, I have weight restored and while I still struggle, I am the best I have been in a long time. Recovery doesn't have a time limit and it isn't linear. This is a process that may take the rest of my life, but I am committed to it. My life is so much more fulfilling now, and I'm no longer surviving, I am living.

I gave myself a try and it changed my life, and now I am asking you to do the same for you.

Where to find the author!

- The Recovery Club podcast available on spotify and apple podcasts

Instagram:

@emilydonoher & @emsinrecovery & @therecoveryclubpodcast

Tiktok: @Emsloveletterz

Email: eatittobeatitpodcast@gmail.com

Printed in Great Britain
by Amazon

18336996R00136